Landscapes of
CORSICA

a countryside guide
Seventh edition

Noel Rochford

SUNFLOWER BOOKS

Seventh edition © 2019
Sunflower Books™
PO Box 36160
London SW7 3WS, UK
www.sunflowerbooks.co.uk

ISBN 978-1-85691-519-9

Fountain on the D81 below Serriera

Important note to the reader

We have tried to ensure that the descriptions and maps in this book are error-free at press date. The book will be updated, where necessary, in future editions. It is always very helpful for us to receive your comments (send them to info@sunflowerbooks.co.uk, please) for the updating of future editions.

We also rely on those who use this book — especially walkers — to take along a good supply of common sense when they explore. Conditions change fairly rapidly on Corsica, and *storms, fires or bulldozing may make a route unsafe at any time*. If the route is not as described, and your way ahead is not secure, return to the point of departure. *Never attempt to complete a tour or walk under hazardous conditions!* Please read carefully the notes on pages 48-53 and the introductory comments at the beginning of each tour and walk (regarding road conditions, equipment, grade, distances and time, etc). Explore *safely*, while at the same time respecting the beauty of the countryside. *And do remember to check for any Updates on our website before you travel!*

Cover photograph: 'Le Coeur' in Les Calanche (Car tour Calvi 1, near Walks 13-15)
Title page: Wild cyclamen in the Forêt de l'Ospédale (Walk 39)

Photographs: Reinhard Baumgärtner (page 122, bottom right); Shutterstock (cover) and pages 4, 12 (top), 20-21, 26-27 (both), 33, 42, 61, 86-87, 88, 110, 116; all other photographs by Noel Rochford and John Underwood
Maps: Sunflower Books. The walking maps have been adapted from the IGN TOP 25 Series (19 sheets covering the whole of Corsica). The relevant sheet numbers are given at the beginning of each walk.
A CIP catalogue record for this book is available from the British Library.
Printed and bound in England: Short Run Press, Exeter

❋ Contents

Santo-Pietro-di-Venaco (Walks 8 and 9)

❂ Preface

Corsica is often referred to as the 'Isle of Beauty', or the 'Scented Isle'; both are very fitting, but I'd like to propose another name: the 'Friendly Isle'. When I went there many years ago to write the first edition of this book, the constant friendliness of the Corsicans towards me outshone all else. Unlike most tourist resorts, it was the rule rather than the exception. Renting an apartment was more like staying with friends than a business affair, and asking for directions ended up in friendly chats, before being lead to my path.

But the other epithets are equally appropriate. No other Mediterranean island can boast such a wealth of natural beauty. Beaches to suit every taste: from long stretches of glaring white sand to pink rocky coves. *Real* mountains — climbers' terrain — that reach almost 3000m/9000ft. In these mountains you stumble upon a magnificent mixture of pine forests, beech woods, chestnut groves, and coppices of evergreen oaks. Streams bound down the mountainsides; rivers cascade through awe-inspiring gorges, leaving behind blue-green pools as clear as crystal. The pink granite hills and cliffs, normally conjured up only for an artist's canvas, are real indeed on Corsica. In spring the countryside is enlivened with a tapestry of wild flowers and maquis in bloom. The hills are ablaze with colour; the air is intoxicatingly scented by the maquis.

For history buffs, the island is littered with evidence of its turbulent past, dating from about 6000BC. Rudimentary megalithic monuments still lie where they were placed thousands of years ago — in fields and out in the maquis-clad hills. The severe and simple Romanesque churches draw you to a halt with the precision of their masonry. Enchanting, story-book villages, many dating from the Middle Ages, adorn the landscape. They perch atop rocky spurs or high on mountain-sides, enjoying belvedere views.

The sheer unspoilt beauty of Corsica is enough to turn anyone into an explorer, be it on foot or by car. Driving around, you get itchy feet just looking at the never-ending beauty spots. You may not be a walker, but you'll soon find yourself wandering off into the countryside. The short walks and picnic suggestions will lure you from your vehicle into the magnetic landscape. Nowhere will you get more pleasure out of walking, whether you choose a short stroll or you tackle the GR20. Driving is equally enjoyable. Corsica is still far from flooded with tourists, as your tours in the countryside will prove. Crossing vast uninhabited tracts of land, you often pass more livestock than vehicles.

Corsica cannot guarantee you the eternal sunshine of, say, the Canaries — or even the prolonged summer of most of the Mediterranean islands. So if it's swimming and sunning you're after, visit Corsica in high season. But if walking is your priority, go in spring for the flowers or in autumn when the trees are turning colour and the shepherds are returning to the valleys with their flocks.

I hope that, armed with *Landscapes of Corsica,* you will discover the real island, and its friendly face.

— NOEL ROCHFORD

Acknowledgements

For help with the preparation of the First and Second editions of this book, warm thanks to the French Tourist Office, L'Agence Régionale du Tourisme, Le Parc Naturel Régional de la Corse, l'Office National des Forêts, and various tourist offices throughout Corsica. Unfortunately I have not been able to return to Corsica for several years. Many thanks to my publishers at Sunflower, John and Pat Underwood, for updating the greatly-revised Third edition and all subsequent editions.

Recommended books and maps

Guides
Eyewitness Guide to Corsica (Dorling Kindersley)
Guide Vert: Corse (Michelin, in French)

Guides only available on Corsica, in French
Le Guide Corse de la Corse
Parc Naturel Régional de la Corse guides to the island's flora, etc
Office National des Forêts guides to forestry walks

Background reading
Dorothy Carrington: *Granite Island: a portrait of Corsica* (Penguin)

Maps
For touring: Michelin map No 345 (*Corse-du-Sud, Haute-Corse*); scale 1:150,000
For walking: IGN 'Top 25' maps (scale 1:25,000; 19 sheets covering the whole of Corsica); available from your local map stockist and in bookshops, kiosks and petrol stations all over the island

Most walks on the island are well signposted: this is the starting point for Walk 36 at the Col de Bavella.

🌻 Getting about

Corsica is a large island indeed, and the public transport network is limited, especially outside high season. The problem is best solved by hiring a vehicle for either part or all of your visit. Some package holidays have very good **fly/drive** arrangements, so do investigate these.

The SNCF runs a good **train** service connecting Ajaccio, Corte, l'Ile-Rousse, Calvi, and Bastia. This is an excellent way to see the interior of the island and reach the mountain walks. The railway tracks and rolling stock have been thoroughly modernised, with comfortable seating and large windows, ideal for sightseeing.

Local **buses** are always fun, but are few and far between. Tourists will find them mostly unsuitable, since scheduling serves the needs of the local community (eg, mail or school buses). In the high season (July to September), however, there are some special 'tourist route' buses which are more helpful for getting about — although not necessarily for getting to and from walks.

Taxis are another way of getting around Corsica. They are very expensive, however, and only economical when shared by a few people. Agree on a price before setting out, and don't be afraid to bargain.

Coach tours may appeal to some of you: you will get to see the major tourist sights and routes in comfort, with the minimum effort.

Timetables for the buses and trains used for the walks in this book are printed on the back of the touring map; due to space limitations*, we have been unable to include timetables for *all* public transport operating on the island. Remember, too, that no timetable in a book can ever be as up-to-date as one you can obtain from the local tourist offices (bus timetables) or the SNCF railway station nearest your base. So when you arrive on Corsica, *do* call in at the railway and tourist offices, where you can arm yourself not only with timetables, but with all manner of helpful reading material.

One of the nicest things about getting around Corsica is the availability of good maps!

---

*For the same reason we have not included any town plans, preferring to use the space to describe more walks. There are excellent plans on the Michelin map recommended opposite — or use your smartphone app.

❀ Touring

Hiring a vehicle (car, motorbike, moped) is the only way really to see Corsica. *Do* check your vehicle thoroughly before setting out, and don't take it if you're not happy with it! Verify all the rental and insurance conditions *in English*, and make sure you understand them. Carry the rental firm's *24-hour telephone numbers* with you. If you pay by credit card, check the amount you sign for and keep all receipts!

The touring notes are brief: they include little history or information about the towns; all this is freely available from local tourist information offices. Instead, I've concentrated on the 'logistics' of touring: times and distances, road conditions, and seeing parts of Corsica that most tourists miss. Most of all, I emphasise possibilities for **walking** and **picnicking**.

Drive carefully, watching for **oncoming cars** (Corsicans habitually drive in the centre of the road until they see an approaching car), **foraging livestock** (especially on mountain roads), and **cyclists** (who are not obliged by law to travel in single file). There are frequent police checks, so keep to the **speed limits** (110km/h on the few dual carriageways, 90km/h on main roads, 70km/h on other roads — reducing to 50km/h or 30km/h in built-up areas). **Allow enough time**: I have only included brief stops at viewpoints labelled 🎦. Many **petrol stations**, especially inland, will be **closed on Sundays/holidays** … even on Saturday afternoons! Take along warm clothing and some food and drink, and **be prepared for delays** on mountain roads (where passes may be closed in bad weather).

The fold-out touring map is designed to be held out opposite the touring notes and contains all the information you need outside the towns. **The tours** (based on Ajaccio, Calvi, Bastia, and Porto-Vecchio) are **numbered in order of importance** (thus, if your time is limited, 'Calvi 1' would be the most highly recommended tour from Calvi).

The **symbols** used in the text correspond to those in the touring map key. But in the interest of clarity, we have *not* put *all* these symbols on the map itself; hotels, restaurants and petrol stations, for example, only appear on the touring map if they are in an *isolated location*.

Short walks and picnic suggestions

Corsica is unbeatable for picnicking, with hundreds of natural, unspoiled locations. There are also some official picnic sites with tables, benches and fountains; those on or near the touring routes have been highlighted in the notes and on the touring map with a ⊼.

Several of my favourite picnic spots are near the car tours and are ideal for stretching your legs. These are mentioned at the top of each tour and at the appropriate place in the touring notes. For a full description, turn to the relevant walk (the picnic spot will be highlighted on the *walking* map with the symbol *P*). Unless you like to picnic just by your car, remember to wear sensible shoes; if the picnic spot is not in shade, take a sunhat with you. A plastic sheet is a good idea, too, in case the ground is damp or prickly. While some of my short walk/picnic suggestions may not be suitable during a long car tour, you may see a landscape that you would like to explore at leisure another day.

Fill your hamper with the exquisite local cheeses (*brocciu* is a good one), *charcutérie* (try *coppa* and *lonzu*), fresh fruit, *embrocciata* (a cheese tartlet) and of course some wine and *local* spring water (like St-Georges, Zilia, or Orezza).

All motorists and picnickers should read the Country code on page 52 and go quietly in the countryside. *Bon appetit!*

The Plage de l'Ostriconi (Walk 20), backed by the hills of the Désert des Agriates. You could picnic on the coastal path, or by the little wooden footbridge that crosses the lagoon (Etang de Foce).

Ajaccio 1: THE PINK CLIFFS OF THE PORTO GULF AND THE SPELUNCA GORGE

Ajaccio • Piana • Porto • Ota • Evisa • Vico • Ajaccio

Some narrow winding roads are followed on this tour. The D81 between Piana and Porto is very narrow and congested with tour coaches and camper vans, and in some places there are steep, unprotected drops; if you do the tour in the direction I describe, this will be no problem, as you will be on the inland side of the road. Watch out for foraging animals on all inland roads. No petrol stations between Porto and Vico (48km). In early spring and late autumn some mountain passes may be closed. Reckon on 210km/130mi, about 7h driving.

En route: Walks 2, 10, 11, 13, 14, 15; Walk 1 is nearby. Picnic suggestions for Walks 1, 10, 13, 14

This tour is packed with unsurpassed coastal scenery. The pink cliffs of the Golfe de Porto are by no means overrated, nor are the intriguing crags of Les Calanche. The great inland valleys, with their chestnut and oak forests, will entice you back another day — perhaps for a picnic, a debauchery of local food and superb scenery.

Leave Ajaccio heading north on the N194 (CALVI PAR LA COTE), at the large roundabout before **Mezzavia** take the first exit (the D31 ring road). Go straight over three roundabouts and, at the fourth, again go straight over — on the D81 for CALVI PAR LA COTE. The towering Rocher des Gozzi, shown on page 58, bulges out of the hills on your right, capturing your attention. Walk 2 would take you to the summit, from where there is one of the finest outlooks in the vicinity. Appietto, the starting point for the walk, is signposted off right at the **Col de Listincone** crossroads (D581; 13km).

Climbing over the squat hills that block out the Golfe de Sagone, you look down onto verdant fields lining the valley that empties in the tiny Golfu di Lava. Scarlet poppies, violet bugloss, dandelions and indigo vetch turn the roadside into a garden. You cross a saddle, the **Bocca San Bastiano**, and meet with a striking panorama (⌨🅿). First you'll see hills stepping their way inland to the 'master peaks' — glimmering white beacons, when still capped in snow. Then the Sagone Gulf distracts you, with its exquisite generous bays of white sand and turquoise water. You pass through a trickle of tourist hamlets and above the vast untouched beach that sits at the mouth of the Liamone River. **Sagone** (38km 🏠🏠🛖△✕🅿), the junction for Evisa and Vico, follows. Turn left to keep along the coastal D81, which has

View from the D81 over the Porto Gulf and Genoese tower

narrowed considerably by now. Further around the gulf, you look back onto the outstretched arm of the Capo di Feno. Soon you're in **Cargèse** (52km ⚕ ⛺ ⛺ △ ✕). The village is stepped up a hillside overlooking a cove. This small resort was founded by Greeks, and Roman and Greek Catholic churches face each other in the centre; the latter contains some 17th-century icons.

Your entry into **Piana** (72km ⛺ ⛺ ⛺ ✕ 🖵) could not be more grand: coming down from the hills, you look straight across the majestic **Porto Gulf ★** (📷), perhaps the most beautiful in the whole of Europe. This natural harbour of pink granite cliffs rising out of an intensely blue sea is spellbinding. Small green coves sit back in the cliffs. And Piana, perched high above the sea, soaks up this unparalleled panorama. Let's do some exploring. On coming into the village, drive past the first hotel. Then fork left on a narrow, *precipitous* lane, up to the **Saliccio Belvedere ★** (📷). From this viewing point you look out to the mountainous interior and over the eroded rocks of Les Calanche. Hidden in the sheer cliffs below is the tiny cove of Ficajola and, if you drive down to it, you will have a splendid view into the Calanche: to get there, return to the D81 and turn off left just before the church (signposted ARONE/MARINE DE FICAJOLA). One kilometre along, take the first turning right and zigzag down a *very narrow road* to **Ficajola ★**, from where a path drops you down into this memorable cove. Prefer beach swimming? Return to the turn-off and continue some 10km

Above: view southwest over Evisa — towards Ota and the peaks shown on page 76. Right: Walk 13 begins at the 'Dog's Head' (Tête du Chien) on the D81 and takes you past spectacular rock formations (see photograph page 78).

further, towards PLAGE D'ARONE. This exhilarating drive carries you past **Capo Rosso★**, a mountain of rock hanging off the southern arm of the gulf, adorned by a Genoese watchtower. When the road forks, keep left to the **Plage d'Arone** (91km).

From the Plage d'Arone, return to Piana and continue north on the D81. Walks 14 and 15 begin just over 1km outside Piana, where a lane turns up right to a car park and football pitch ('STADE MUNICIPAL' and PARKING SIGN). You're now winding through the pink world of **Les Calanche★** (📷). Guy de Maupassant described it as a 'forest of purple granite'. Walks 13-15 explore the Calanche in depth. Why not stretch your legs on Walk 14, which begins here, its alternative version from **Les Roches Bleues** 1.6km further north, or Walk 13 from the signposted **Tête du Chien** another 0.6km further on?

Out of this 'jungle' of rock, you pass some pine-shaded picnic spots (no facilities except rubbish bins). The gulf reappears, and Porto comes into view. It sits in a poster-like setting★, best appreciated from above: the rich colour contrasts of the pale-grey pebble beach, blue sea, green vegetation and rose-coloured rock shoreline are a rare sight. **Porto** (114km ⌂ ▲▲▲✕⌂⌂), built solely for tourism, is overlooked by a square Genoese watchtower. Continuing past the village, turn inland, swinging sharply back to the right on the D124 towards OTA. Ascending into the deep Porto Valley, you come into olive trees. Spring-green chestnut groves stand out in the dark cloak of the surrounding vegetation.

Ota (119km ▲▲▲✕⌂; Walks 10 and 11) is an impressive sight. The village, shown opposite and on page 76, is perched high on the hillside amidst olive trees. Pink craggy walls tower overhead. Bump your way down to the **Ponte Vecchiu ★** (⌂), the beautifully-restored Genoese foot-bridge eventually seen ahead. This is a perfect picnic spot, where you can take an invigorating swim … but expect company — it's in all the guides. A minute later you cross 'les Deux Ponts d'Ota', two enchanting stone bridges at the confluence of the Onca River and the **Gorges de Spelunca ★**. A path on the left, just beyond the second bridge, would take you up the gorge to another lovely picnic spot in 30 minutes — the Genoese Pont de Zaglia (see Short walk 10, page 73; photograph page 74).

Climbing to a junction, turn *very sharply* left on the D84 for Evisa. The road swings back into another gorge full of chestnut groves. At the sign denoting the entrance to **Evisa** (137km ▲▲▲△✕), a viewpoint in the cemetery on the left (⌂) gives you a last opportunity to capture all this beauty with a photograph. Walk 10 begins here.

Turn sharp right on the D70 at the junction beyond Evisa. From the **Col de Sevi** (1101m/3610ft ⌂), you enjoy a fine view back over the Tavulella Valley. On the descent, an immense valley (the Gorges de Liamone) opens up on your left, dominated by the Punta di a Spusata. Turn left into **Vico** (159km ▲▲△✕⌂). A few hundred metres from the junction, fork right to the Couvent de St-François (✝). A wood-carving of Christ in the 15th-century church is claimed to be the oldest on Corsica. Vico is a village full of character, with tall granite buildings lining its alleys and single main street.

To complete the circuit, return to the D70 and follow it back to **Sagone**. You drop down through wooded hills to the Sagone Valley floor. Lush pastures fill the river flat. Alders trickle along the stream banks. In May the fields are flooded with deep blue *Echium* — a dazzling sight. From Sagone head left on the D81 to **Ajaccio** (210km).

Ajaccio 2: COUNTRY ROADS TO BASTELICA

Ajaccio • Porticcio • Coti-Chiavari • Bastelica • Gorges du Prunelli • Tolla • Ajaccio

*The roads are variable, generally narrow and winding. The stretches between Marato and the Col St-Georges and Bastelica and Tolla are **exceptionally narrow**; some people will find them vertiginous. Be alert for foraging animals on inland roads. No petrol stations between Porticcio and Bastelicaccia (117km). Reckon on 174km/108mi, 7h driving.*

En route: Walks 1, 3 (both with short walk and picnic suggestions)

Get out into the countryside and savour rural Corsica, an island where much of the land remains untamed, covered in maquis and a wealth of forests. In springtime you will be overwhelmed by the extravaganza of wild flowers illuminating the hills. The highlight of this tour is the jade-green Tolla Reservoir. But don't be too late returning to Ajaccio for the fire of pink sunset over the Iles Sanguinaires!

Follow the N196 dual carriageway east to the PORTICCIO roundabout (11.5km) and turn right on the D55 to **Porticcio** (17.5km ▲▲▲△✕♥WC), one of Corsica's largest tourist centres. Its beautiful golden beach and picturesque setting are now the casualties of development. Much of this side of the gulf is 'ritzy-residential'. Following the coast, you curve in and out of pretty bays and coves. Your view extends across the harbour to Ajaccio and the hills behind it.

Approaching Verghia, you skirt the most beautiful beach on this stretch of coast. The long white sand collar curves round towards a stand of pines. If you would like to see the beautiful cork oak wood shown opposite (and, in spring, a deluge of wild flowers) try the short version of Walk 3 and go up into the Forêt Domaniale de Chiavari. This signposted nature trail (Sentier du Myrte) is near the end of the beach (28km), immediately before the bridge over the Ruisseau de Zirione. (The longer version of Walk 3 begins on the far side of the same bridge.)

The main tour continues on the D55, which turns off left less than 1km further on, in **Verghia** (29km ▲▲△✕). Now you climb through a magnificent evergreen forest to a hairpin bend where you keep straight ahead on the D55A to **Coti-Chiavari** (39km ▲▲✕🍴). This small terraced village sits at the foot of a maquis wood, with a fine outlook over the tail of the gulf to the Iles Sanguinaires. Descending from the settlement, you look down onto another tower-crowned headland, the Capu di Muru. Just over 5km beyond Coti-Chiavari, having joined the D155, pass the turn-off for Capu di Muru and bear left.

Splendid coastal views follow you all the way, as you head east over the hills. In the distance, ridges pour down off the island's central spine. Below lies the deeply-indented Baie de Cupabia, with an irresistible, untouched beach. If you're ready

14

for a break, this bay may be just what you're looking for: the turn-off comes up on your right after 53km. The main tour keeps left here towards SERRA-DI-FERRO, then turns left and left again, on the D355 for TASSINCA and AJACCIO.

You climb into the hills, where goats roam wild. Meet the D55 again at the **Col de Gradella**, and turn right. Not far

These lovely cork oaks on the Sentier du Myrte (Short walk 3 and Picnic suggestion) can only be stripped every 10-12 years.

beyond **Marato**, the only village out here in 'the wilds', be sure to take the *second* right-hand turn to continue on the D55 (signposted for ALBITRECCIA/GUARGUALE). Hugging steep rocky hillsides on an exceptionally narrow road lined with dazzling yellow *Coronilla*, you look out over a wooded valley. Keep left all the way to the N196, then turn left, to climb to the **Col St-Georges** (84km ⬤✖️☕).

Descend from the pass and come to the outskirts of **Cauro** (⬤⬤✖️). Turn sharp right on the D27 before entering the village. You meander along a lush valley occupied by small farms and boskets. Soon you disappear into the high hills again and, 4km before you reach Bastelica, you pass by the turn-off left to Tolla (your return route). Perhaps what you'll remember most about **Bastelica** (109.5km ⬤⬤⬤✖️) is the magnificent chestnut wood that surrounds it. Your approach to the village takes you past tired old stone walls that enclose plots and orchards. Some fine old stone mansions are found in the six hamlets that comprise Bastelica, stretching out across the valley inclines. Drive between the houses, then swing back left opposite the church, to return to the Tolla turn-off. Monte Renoso (Corsica's fourth highest peak at 2352m/7715ft) sits high in the valley.

Turn right when you reach the Tolla road (D3), a *very* narrow route cut into the gorge walls. Your homeward route follows the scenic **Gorges du Prunelli**★, a continuation of Bastelica's picturesque valley. Drive *very carefully* and only admire the views where you can pull over off the road *safely*. The river flows far below. Rounding a corner, the gorge opens up, and the jade-green **Lac de Tolla**★ (a reservoir) fills the valley floor. What a view! A collar of pink rock, marking the waterline, separates the sherwood green of the wooded hillsides from the jade-green of the lake. **Tolla** (115.5km ✖️☕) is the village set high on the grassy slopes, overlooking both the dam and the rugged interior. Beyond the village, a lay-by enables you to pull off the road and enjoy the setting (☕). Crossing the **Bocca di Mercujo** (✖️), park at the restaurant and follow the track to the belvedere ★ (☕ 10min downhill) for a more spectacular view of the dam and gorge.

Follow the D3 back to the N196 just beyond **Bastelicaccia** (🚌) and turn right, back to **Ajaccio** (174km). To see the magnificent sunset over the Iles Sanguinaires, go straight through town and follow the coast out to the **Pointe de la Parata**, 12km west (✖️☕; Walk 1 and Picnic suggestion). Find yourself a soft piece of ground and let it all take place...

Ajaccio 3: SOME HISTORY ... AND THE D69

Ajaccio • Col St-Georges • Filitosa • Propriano • Campomoro • Sartène • Aullène • Zicavo • Santa-Maria-Siché • Ajaccio

This is a long and tiring tour, which is best divided into two days — the western side one day and the scenic D69 another. The country roads and the D69 are very narrow and bumpy. All roads are winding; driving will be slow. Watch out for foraging animals. Reckon on 250km/155mi, 10h driving.

En route: No walks or picnic suggestions

This drive is brim-full of magnificent country scenery and at its best in spring, when the meadows are saturated with wild flowers and the trees are freshly green. You dip in and out of gentle farmed valleys interrupted by rocky hills. But as usual, it's the mountain landscape that lures you on: the cosy, welcoming perched villages, the vast woodlands cloaking the slopes, and the far-reaching views as you climb higher and higher, up to where the shepherds graze their flocks. Also en route lie Filitosa and Sartène, two very different glimpses of Corsica's turbulent history — a prehistoric site and a town that clings to tradition.

Leave Ajaccio by heading south on the main N196 towards Propriano. You cross the Prunelli River and climb to the **Col St-Georges** (29km ▲ ✕ ☞). Once over the pass, you look out over an enormous basin of low rolling valleys. Silvery-green olive trees stand out amid evergreen oaks. Cross the Taravo River and soon the woods give way to fields. Pass through **Casalabriva** (57km ▲▲ ✕), then, 1.8km further on, leave the N196: turn sharp right on the D302 to **Sollacaro**, an appealing, rustic village steeped in history. Literature buffs may be interested to know that Dumas' novel, *The Corsican Brothers* (which incidentally has little to do with the island), came out of his short sojourn here in 1841. Boswell also spent some time here in 1765, in the company of Pasquale Paoli, the first and only president of an independent Corsica (1755-68). Just through

Sartène

Sollacaro turn sharp left on the D57, down to an undulating plain spread out along the Taravo delta.

If you're not 'into' history, you won't find the insubstantial **Station Préhistorique de Filitosa** ★ (68km ⛵ ⛰ ✕M) overly exciting. However, compensation enough for nature lovers is the site's picturesque setting and the profusion of wild flowers in spring, especially the clusters of purple orchids. Filitosa is the island's most important prehistoric settlement and amazingly, this site remained undetected for nearly 5000 years. An avenue of pines leads you to the *menhirs* (stone-carved megalithic 'statues' that resemble standing mummies). Cork and olive trees beautify the site, and cows graze nearby. If you read French, you'll find the small museum here of interest.

Following the Taravo, you head towards a coastline sprinkled with holiday homes and tourist hamlets. At a T-junction with the D157 go left for PROPRIANO. Soon your view extends across the Golfe de Valinco to a long inviting stretch of sand at the foot of the Taravo hills — the Plage de Portigliolo. This will be your 'beach stop' later in the tour. Propriano is just across the bay now. Unfortunately, the terminal disease of tourism has already begun to eat away at the setting. Some 5km before the town, you rejoin the N196 and circle behind the beach at **Propriano** (86km ⛰ ⛰ △✕➧⊕). You can either stay on the N196 to visit the town or turn left for SARTENE/BONIFACIO on the D19a bypass. Just beyond the Rizzanèse River, leave the N196 and turn right on the D121, towards the coast. Passing Propriano's Tavaria Aerodrome, the road skirts the superb Plage de Portigliolo, the long beach that you could see from across the bay. A low ridge of sand rises off the aquamarine sea and folds over into green fields. You can park at the end of the beach.

Crossing the hills for Campomoro, you get a stunning panorama over this clear sweeping bay and onto the distant encircling hills. Shortly, the tiny village of **Belvédère** is reached. Perfectly named, this hillside perch has an enviable view (📷) straight out over the harbour. Outside the village head right at the T-junction , to continue on the D121 to **Campomoro** (102km ⛵ ⛰ △✕), set around a shallow beach. A Genoese tower adorns a nearby promontory. Settlement on the maquis-covered hillsides is slowly eroding Campomoro's off-the-beaten-track appeal.

Return to Belvédère and at the junction keep straight ahead on the D21 for GROSSA. You enter an isolated (not to say bleak) countryside drenched in scrub. You bypass Grossa, a handful of stone houses set back off the road. Further on, you circle some farms well ensconced in these wavy hills. The landscape is beautifully untamed, rocky and woven in maquis. Put your head out of the car window and smell the fragrance — a mixture of cistus, lavender and thorny broom. Always keeping to the D21 for SARTENE, you come to a T-junction with the D48. Tizzano (and the prehistoric sites of Cauria and Palaggiu) are to the right. Personally, I found Tizzano (⌂▲▲✕) overrated in many guides, and the main tour doesn't visit it. But both sites are signposted, if you wish to take a detour.

Turn left on the D48 and left again on meeting the N196. Mounting a crest, you come to an excellent panorama over the Rizzanèse Valley's basin of trees and fields. **Sartène** ★ (127km ✝▲▲▲△✕⬛⊕M) terraces a steep hillside. Coming into town, you pass the imposing San Damiano Monastery (✝) and look over a hillside fortified with tall stone buildings. Sartène terraces a steep hillside. It is one of Corsica's most traditional towns, where matters of honour and the vendetta were much in evidence for longer then anywhere else on the island. The place is now best known for its Good Friday 'Procession du Castenacciu', a three hour-long parade of hooded penitents through candle-lit streets, which harks back to medieval times. Climb the steps and wander through the back streets and alleys, sampling the delights of this living history book. The museum of Corsican pre-history houses a wide collection of objects dating back to 6000BC (of particular interest if you visit any sites on this tour). The tree-shaded Place de la Libération is at the heart of the town: here are the town hall (formerly the palace of the Genoese governor) and the 18th-century Eglise Ste-Marie.

If the day hasn't passed you by, from Sartène make for the D69: follow the N196 towards AJACCIO and turn right on the D268 for STE-LUCIE-DE-TALLANO. But don't forget to look back on Sartène! Just over 4km along, look out left for the arched **Spin'a Cavallu** ★ (the 'Horse's Back'; ⬛ ⍊), a beautifully restored 13th-century Genoese bridge (*not signposted;* parking opposite). Heading inland, you pass pastures knee-high in grass and speckled with red, purple and yellow flowers. On reaching the first junction, turn left on the D69 for AULLÈNE, crossing the Rizzanèse.

An intriguing countryside opens up before you. The Rizzanèse twists its way through the central massif. A few lone houses enjoy the solitude of this cut-off valley. Small stone bridges and the ever-present wild flowers add to the countryfied charm. The

D69 takes you into **Aullène** (163km ▲✕▣). Set amidst chestnut groves and silhouetted against a cone-shaped mountain, this village curves around the crest of a ridge.

From Aullène follow signs for ZICAVO (still D69). Leaving the trees behind, you climb into cowherds' domain — a bleak, rocky landscape with meagre pastureland scattered amongst the heather-clad slopes. Humble farm dwellings have been converted into attractive summer retreats. Crossing the **Col de la Vaccia** (▣), you have a wonderful view back across this elevated valley onto Aullène, comfortably set in the woodlands below. To the west lies the deep Taravo Valley and, all around you, a choppy sea of hills and mountains. Descending, you come into splendid beech woods; under the evening sun the leaves glow and the hills come alight. Around here, be sure to search the roadside for exquisite mountain anemones. Their colour varies from off-white or pale mauve to blue. You may also spot clumps of almost-fluorescent pale-green hellebores.

You cross over the roaring cascade shown above just before entering **Zicavo** (189km ▲✕). At the Y-fork as you come into the top of the village, keep left on the D757a for AJACCIO and STA-MARIE-SICHE. A narrow wooded gorge leads you out of this enclosed valley, and you briefly follow the Taravo River once more. At the junction 4km downhill, turn sharp left for AJACCIO.

Some 2.4km further on, in the pretty tree-lined village of **Bains de Guitera** (195km ▲✕▣), fork right for AJACCIO (D83).

Climbing up through forested valleys, you cross yet another pass. Rustic, shuttered villages, all picturesquely located, lie along your homeward route: some cling to ridges, some adorn prominent crags, and some shelter in hollows. A couple of kilometres before rejoining the N196, you come to the farming village of **Sta-Maria-Siché** (216km ▮▲✕▣). Watch for the 15th-century Château d'Ornano, set in the trees just below the village. Once back on the N196, turn right: a straight run of 34km takes you to **Ajaccio** (250km).

Calvi's citadel under a setting sun

Calvi 1: THE ISOLATED NIOLO BASIN AND THE BREATHTAKING WESTERN GULFS

Calvi • l'Ile-Rousse • Ponte Leccia • Col de Vergio • Evisa • Gorges de Spelunca • Ota • Porto • Calvi

Beyond Ponte Leccia driving will be slow: the route is winding and often narrow. Always be on the alert for foraging animals! The weather can be cold and cloudy (much of the route is quite high); the Col de Vergio may be closed in bad weather. There are no petrol stations between l'Ile-Rousse and Ponte Leccia (41km) or Calacuccia and Porto (51km). Since this is such a long drive, I have omitted Les Calanche; allow another full day for exploring the environs of the Porto Gulf (use the notes for 'Ajaccio 1'). I highly recommend doing this tour in the direction described (especially if you have nervous passengers), due to the narrow roads beyond Porto. Reckon on 237km/147mi, about 7h30min driving.

En route: Walks 10, 11, 12, 16, 17, 18, 19, 20; Walks 24, 25 and 26 are nearby. Picnic suggestions for Walks 10, 12, 17, 18, 20 and 24

Crossing the island's central spine of mountains, you pass through the isolated Niolo Basin, home of shepherds and herdsmen. On your return to the west coast, you climb to the Col de Vergio, the highest road pass on Corsica (1477m). You can cool off in the fresh limpid pools of the Aitone or Spelunca gorges, before descending to the beautiful gulfs of Porto and Girolata.

From Calvi take the N197 (the main north road for l'Ile-Rousse and Bastia). Crossing the plain, you look up to the pretty hillside village of **Lumio**★ (9.5km ✚🏔🏠⛺🍴; photograph page

31), terracing the hills of Capu d'Occi and Capu Bracajo. It commands a fine view over the Calvi Gulf and the citadel. Pass 'Chez Charles' (where Walk 18 ends and Alternative walk 18 begins) and, at the junction, keep left on the N197 to continue along the coast. You drive above Marine de Sant' Ambrogio (▲▲☙✕), a classy resort, and then Algajola (16km ⌂☗▲▲▲△ ✕🏠), another major resort, at the end of a curving bay. Its Genoese fort is in ruins, except for the citadel. Inland, Monte Grosso dominates the great wall of mountains.

You pass several roads leading inland to the Balagne (Car tour 'Calvi 3'). Then, just before l'Ile-Rousse, you pass the striking and least spoilt beach along this stretch of coast, the **Plage de Botre**, sitting off the turquoise-blue Baie de Guinchetu. All you see of **l'Ile-Rousse** (23km ☗ ▲▲▲△✕🏠⊕🖼WC) is a street lined with plane trees. Save your visit to this very pleasant town (photographs pages 31 and 91) for the day you do Walk 19, which ends here.

Further along the coast your views extend to the more rugged shore line of the Désert des Agriates and, in the distance, Cap Corse. Beyond the entrance to the **Parc de Saleccia** (27km ❀), you skirt the extensive sandy beach of **Lozari** (30km) and keep along the wide coastal road (now the N1197, 'la Balanina'). The road swings inland above the lovely landscape shown on pages 8-9 — the unspoilt **Plage de l'Ostriconi** (Walk 20). At the next junction, ignore the D81 left to St-Florent and Bastia; keep along the Ostriconi Valley on the N1197 for Ponte Leccia.

At **Ponte Leccia** (67km ▲▲▲△✕🏠), a major junction, you join the N193. Carry on past **Francardo** (off to the right at 76km; ▲▲✕) and, just after crossing the Golo, turn right on the D84 for CALACUCCIA. The Golo, Corsica's great 84km-long river, runs along on your right. Recrossing the river after 6km, keep left at the T-junction. You enter a magnificent gorge, the **Scala di Sta Regina ★**, a winding passageway that links the Niolo with the east. Rocky hillsides tumble off the towering mountain chain that rises some 1000m/3300ft on either side. Approaching the **Niolo ★**, the gorge opens out, and rough pastures appear. Remains of stone walls, footbridges, and solitary huts speak of grazing land.

At the roundabout just before you enter Calacuccia, fork left on the D218b for CASAMACCIOLI and circle the picturesque **Barrage de Calacuccia**. You cross the dam wall and look over the reservoir to the amphitheatre of rocky mountains that encloses this high basin. Sloping pastures lie between the scattering of sheltered hamlets and the crags. Monte Cinto (Corsica's highest peak at 2706m/8875ft) stands out with its ramp-shaped summit. **Casamaccioli** (100km ☗▲) is a pretty village set back off the wooded banks of the lake. Every year on the 8th of September, the island's most important festival is held here (the Nativity of the Virgin). All the shepherds return from the mountains with their flocks for this three-day fête.

At the T-junction just inside Casamaccioli, turn right and continue around the lake. Returning to **Calacuccia** (105km ✚🏔✗🍽), at the T-junction turn left for *ALBERTACCE*. Calacuccia is quite ordinary, but superbly sited overlooking the lake. In the church there is an interesting 17th-century wooden statue of Christ; the carving is particularly expressive. Continuing on the D84, you pass below a 17th-century Franciscan monastery (✚) set back in the trees. Beyond **Albertacce** (107km 🏔 and **M** of archaeology) you cross the Golo for the last time (📷). Note the small footbridge below left and the pretty gorge cutting back up to the right.

As you head across the plateau, the landscape becomes noticeably rocky and is clad in trees and bushes. Soon pines take over, and you're in the **Forêt de Valdu Niellu ★**, Corsica's largest forest (🌲). Some of these pencil-straight trees reach a

Brightly-blooming hillsides: late spring in the Niolo

height of 50m/165ft. Pull over at a roadside viewpoint (📷), to look back down the bowl-shaped Golo Valley to the dam. Still climbing, come to the ski station and the highest hotel on the island (🏔️✕). Approaching the **Col de Vergio ★** (📷; 1477m/ 4845ft), you catch a glimpse of Punta Licciola and, behind it, the 'pierced' summit of Capu Tafunatu — one of the focal points on Walk 25 (photograph page 102). From the pass there are more splendid views towards the Licciola peak and other bare summits, all lightly flecked with a luminous green lichen, and down over the Golo. The Col de Vergio straddles the island's north/south border (Haute-Corse and Corse-du-Sud), two very different and mutually antagonistic cultures. The statue of Christ here, with its reconciliatory subtext, 'Love one another as I have loved you', was the inspiration of Evisa's priest.

Two versions of Walk 12, each with picnic suggestions, are possible as you follow the winding Aitone Valley seaward. The first, the Sentier de la Sittelle, starts at a parking area on the right 5.5km down from the col. The second, the Chemin des Châtaigniers, 3.5km further on (by fire-point sign 'EVI05'), leads to the **Cascades d'Aitone ★**.

Out of the forest, you enter chestnut groves. Turn right at the junction and head into **Evisa** (133km 🏔️🏔️🏠△✕), a charming mountain village, well placed for exploring the interior and the Porto Gulf area. Walk 10 sets out from here. At the sign for the village exit, don't miss the viewpoint in the cemetery on the right (📷) towards Ota, perched high in the deep Porto Valley. The rocky hillsides here blush pink, and pinnacles of rock burst up out of the surrounding walls. The road curls down into a side valley thick with chestnut trees. Keep right past two turn-offs left for Marignana; then, 14km from Evisa, be prepared for a *very sharp right turn* onto the single-lane D124 for Ota. You soon cross the Porto River, at the mouth of the **Gorges de Spelunca ★**. There are two good picnicking choices here, both by Genoese foot-bridges: see the Short walk/picnic suggestion on page 73 and photographs on page 74. A few hundred metres beyond 'les Deux Ponts d'Ota' ('Ota's Two Bridges', where there is usually enough room to park), you look down onto the lovely, high-arched **Ponte Vecchiu ★** (📷), one of the suggested picnic settings. The river here is ideal for swimming.

This narrow road has carried us to **Ota** (148km 🏔️🏔️🏠✕📷), the colourful village with bright orange-tiled rooftops shown on pages 12 and 76. A lofty ridge capped in rose-coloured rock looms above it. Walk 10 ends here, and Walk 11 begins here. Leaving the valley, you come down to the tourist village of Porto (Tour 'Ajaccio 1'). This tour doesn't enter Porto; instead, turn right at the junction, on the D81. From here you have the superb view of Porto ★ and its spectacular setting shown on pages 10-11. The rock dome of the Capu d'Orto, behind you, stands guard over the bay. Superb seascapes open up over the headlands. Twin-headed Monte Seninu rises straight up out of the sea, dramatically punctuating the end of the gulf. A vast beach, the **Plage de Bussaglia** (▲▲▲△✕), appears below. Watch for the lovely fountain shown on page 2 near the turning right to Serriera. Beautiful eucalyptus trees line the way to **Partinello** (with a similar fountain at the end of the village).

Continue along the corniche to the **Bocca di a Croce** ★ (✕). Pull over to the parking area *carefully* (dangerous bend) and continue on foot to the viewpoint (📷). The pretty cove of Girolata sits tucked back in a striking stretch of coast. Shorter walk 26 *(highly recommended)* leads from this pass to Girolata via the Anse de Tuara, an exquisite cove (notes page 103; photograph page 104).

Some 12km further on you cross the **Col de Palmarella**; the road widens and descends into the flat-bottomed Fango Valley. This is the setting for Short walk 24 so, when you tire of beaches, one day take the D351 up into this peaceful valley, find yourself your own rock pool, and enjoy a lazy day of swimming, sunning and picnicking. This unbelievably lovely setting, with a riverbed ranging in colour from pink to purple, and blue and green river pools, is a particular favourite of mine (see Short walk/picnic suggestion on page 98; photos on pages 98,100).

Turn left down the valley, then right for CALVI. (But first, if you have time, continue left on the D351 to **Galéria** (🏠▲▲▲△✕), where Walk 26 begins.) Park on the right after 3km, just below the tower. Then walk down to the beach at the mouth of the Fango, a UNESCO-protected area, with its pretty lagoon and enchanting coppice.

The main tour continues on the D81 by crossing the Fango. At the junction, turn left along the longer and *narrower,* but far prettier coastal route (D81b), with fine views back over the Golfe de Galéria. Coming into **l'Argentella** (214km ▲▲△✕), you look out over the Baie de Crovani. L'Argentella sits on the edge of an open valley, sheltered by a sweeping curve of rocky hills. Back along the coast, your views reach to la Revellata, the arm of land with the lighthouse (Walk 16; photograph page 83). Having rounded the turquoise-green **Baie de Nichiareto**, you enjoy an amazing vista of fat rocky mountains in shades of pink, orange and grey. Looking out over the jagged sea cliffs serrating the coastline, you pass the turn-off to the chapel of Notre Dame de la Serra★ (✝📷; photographs page 85), one of the settings for Walks 16 and 17 — a delightful place for an evening picnic under a lowering sun. Now **Calvi** is just 4km away (237km).

Calvi 2: THE ASCO VALLEY

Calvi • l'Ile-Rousse • Haut Asco • Asco • Calvi

The road is good as far as the Asco turn-off, but the D147 to Asco narrows to only one lane in places. You may not be able to get as far as Haut Asco in early spring or late autumn. It can also be very cold and misty on this high road. Watch for foraging animals. Ponte Leccia, 2km beyond the Asco turn-off, is your last chance for petrol for 62km. Reckon on 192km/119mi, 6h driving.

En route: Walks 18, 19, 20. Picnic suggestions for Walks 18 and 20

The Asco Valley is one of those gorges that disappears into the interior mountains and then stops dead in its tracks at the foot of towering crags. Paths to attract the curious and energetic abound here, so take a picnic lunch and spend an hour or two somewhere on the edge of the beautiful river that keeps you company all the way up. Then, before the sun has lost its warmth, head back to the Genoese bridge below Asco and revive yourself in the blue-green pool that it spans. Shake the ice off and make for Calvi under a dying sun.

Follow the notes for Car tour 'Calvi 1' all the way to the turn-off for the **Gorges de l'Asco★** (65km; 2km north of Ponte Leccia). Turn right (D47) and, 5km further on, keep left on the D147 (where the D47 heads off right to Moltifao). Soon great salients of rock loom above. Further along, the abruptness subsides, and the walls lean back to reveal side valleys. Asco (82km) soon comes into sight, built on terraces in the steep valley wall. Without entering the village, swing up right towards the ski station. You come into a magnificent

pine forest, the Forêt de Carozzica, as you skirt the gushing Stranciacone River (many good picnic spots and room to park).

Haut Asco (93km ▲▲🛆✕), the ski station, is a bit of an eyesore, but the surrounding alpine scenery is enchanting. It's best to scramble up the slopes until the hotel is out of sight! A breathtaking 30-minute climb would take you past grand Corsican pines and up to a plateau strewn with pink and mauve rock, amongst the foothills of **Monte Cinto★**.

If you fancy a dip in the pool below Asco on your return, head right at the Y-fork as you approach the village (where the D147 is signed left to Ponte Leccia) and then go sharp right again, to zigzag down a narrow

Bridge below Asco and (above right): Moltifao, a village on the 'roller coaster' optional return route

lane to the bridge (swimming is officially banned here, but no one takes any notice). Visit **Asco**, a village dating from the 11th century, then return to **Calvi** the same way (192km). Or try the 'roller-coaster' D47 via Moltifao and, at the T-junction, turn left on the D547, to cross the Capanna Pass and descend to the N197.

Calvi 3: VILLAGES OF THE BALAGNE, AND THE TARTAGINE VALLEY

Calvi • Calenzana • Muro • Speloncato • Bocca di a Battaglia • Tartagine Valley • Belgodère • l'Ile-Rousse • Corbara • Sant' Antonino • Lumio • Calvi

Most of the tour follows narrow, winding roads. Watch out for foraging animals, especially between Speloncato and Belgodère. There are no reliably open petrol stations between Calenzana and l'Ile-Rousse (115km). The Bocca di a Battaglia might be closed in early spring or late autumn in bad weather. Reckon on 161km/100mi; 6h driving.

En route: Walks 18, 19, 21; Walks 22-24 are accessible from Calenzana via the D51, but are best reached via the airport road (D81) and then the D251 direct to Bonifatu. Picnic suggestions for Walks 18, 19, 22

The Balagne is a region full of charming villages. Every one seems to have its own baroque church, and all have a balcony view over the plains and hills that characterise the area. Stopping at all of them is impossible, and choosing between them a difficult task. I'll leave that to you. Over the hills, behind this salubrious countryside, lies a quiet, cut-off valley that few people visit, the Tartagine. Its beautiful pine and evergreen oak forests, and the finely-etched Monte Padro, make another lovely circuit, before you return through the Balagne to Calvi.

Follow the Ile-Rousse road (N197) out of Calvi for 4.5km, then turn right at the roundabout on the D151 to **Calenzana** (12.5km ✝🏔⛺⛪🔺✕🅿). Set in a flat valley amidst olive and almond trees, with its back to the prominent Monte Grosso (1938m/ 6355ft), Calenzana verges on being a town, with its maze of alleys, gardens and shops. It's an important agricultural centre, noted for ewes'-milk cheese *(brocciu)*, wine, and *charcu-*

Speloncato from the D63 to Olmi-Cappella

Sant' Antonino — masterpiece of the Balagne

térie. The 17th/18th-century baroque church of St-Blaise, shown on page 94, dwarfs the village centre; its elegant campanile enhances the square. Walk 21 begins here. Just over 1km outside the village, still on the D151, is the tiny church dedicated to Ste-Restitude (✝), a Corsican martyr beheaded by the Romans in 303.

The road winds deeper into the Fiume Seccu Valley, through untidy countryside crammed with olive, oak, cherry and chestnut trees. An enchanting old stone church stands above the road in **Lunghignano** (22km ✝✕). **Montemaggiore** (23.5km ✝📷) adorns a prominent rocky ridge jutting out into the Fiume Seccu. It commands a fine view over Calvi's gulf. A kilometre out of the village, just where the D151 swings up left, take the dirt track off right, to the simple 12th-century Romanesque church of St-Rainer (✝), resting in fields. Back on the main road and climbing into cistus-covered hills, you have expansive views over the settings for Walks 16 and 17: the plains below, the Calvi Gulf, la Revellata, and the hills of rock that enclose the Figarella Valley. Then, crossing the **Bocca di Salvi ★** (📷), you look down into the Algajola basin, chequered with fields. Sant' Antonino is perched high on the crest of a ridge ahead.

On meeting an intersection, turn right on the D71 for Belgodère (there is ☎ off to the left here, not always open). The sickle-shaped Codole Reservoir stretches out in the floor of the Regino Valley. After 4km, fork right on the D13 into **Muro** (33km ✝✕📷); you arrive at the door of the imposing church, the Eglise de l'Annonciation, one of the finest examples of the

baroque style on Corsica. Continue past the church to leave
Muro and turn right for FELICETO when you meet the D71 again.
Feliceto (39km ♙✖) is surrounded by orchards. Ignore the
fork right to Nessa, but at the next Y-fork head right on the D663
for SPELONCATO, strategically sited on a high outcrop of rock
overlooking the Regino basin. Now you ascend for some fine
views over **the Balagne ★**.

Squeezing through the narrow streets of **Speloncato** (45km
♱♙♟✖☺), leave on the lane just to the right of the *Poste,* the
narrow D63 to Olmi-Cappela *(not usually signposted)*. Climb
past a derelict monastery and the view shown on page 28 to the
Bocca di a Battaglia ★ (☺✖). Here an even more stupendous
panorama unfolds — over the reservoir, Speloncato, the
embroidery of fields in the Regino Valley, the luminous green
Lozari Bay, the arid Désert des Agriates, Cap Corse, and the red
Ile-Rousse.

You drop down into a tree-flooded valley. On reaching the
D963, turn sharp right, then keep right for the rest of the way.
The bumpy road winds high above the Melaja and **Tartagine ★**
valleys. Monte Padro (2390m/7840ft) dominates the landscape
on your left. Beyond a shuttered forestry house, you cross the
Tartagine, a healthy stream with knee-deep pools. The road ends
at private property (parking area), but enticing paths lead into
the forest.

Turn back and, always keeping to the D963, continue straight
through **Olmi-Cappela**. When you eventually meet the N197,
turn left for l'Ile-Rousse. You pass high above Palasca, a lonely
village nestled round its church. You might like to visit the imposing 13th-century Church of St-Thomas at **Belgodère**
(112km ☐♱✖☺WC), another strategically-sited village. From
the scant remains of the fortress that once dominated the
settlement, you look down over the Regino and Prato valleys.
Circling down above the fertile plains, you pass the turn-off to
Regino and Lozari's tempting beach.

Head straight through **l'Ile-Rousse** (128km ♱♙♟△✖☐
☺WC), where Walk 19 ends; it certainly deserves a visit, but is
easily accessible by train from Calvi. At the large 'Leclerc'
roundabout outside the town, take the third exit (CALVI, LUMIO)
and then go left immediately on the D151 for CORBARA. From
the hillside, the Baie de Guinchetu and the Plage de Botre look
enticing. Turn left again at the next fork (still the D151).

From the moment you see **Corbara** (132km ♱✖☺ WC),
you know it's going to be different. Palm trees in a garden above
the road set the scene. There's a distinct Moorish flavour about
the place. From the chapel of Notre Dame (built into the rocky
vertex above the village and once the site of the Castel de

Left: churches in Lumio (top) and Aregno; right: l'Ile-Rousse

Corbara), you have fine views over Algajola Bay to la Revellata. The 18th-century Church of the Annunciation stands guard over the village.

Continuing round the Algajola basin on the D151 for PIGNA, with good views of Corbara's setting, you pass some magnificent family tombs, then spot the imposing 15th-century Monastery of Corbara ★ (✝) below Monte Sant' Angelo. **Pigna** (134km) crowns a hillock growing out of the valley wall. The village is a handicraft centre ★, where traditional arts such as weaving, pottery, and woodworking are practised.

A profusion of olive and citrus trees welcomes you to **Aregno** (137km ✝). On your left you pass one of the area's masterpieces: the 12th-century Pisan Romanesque Eglise de la Trinité ★. Do stop to see the humourous figures decorating the façade and two exquisite 15th-century frescoes. Then, just 1km beyond Aregno, *turn sharp left* (D413) for the 'pièce de résistance' of the Balagne, **Sant' Antonino** ★ (141km ✕⌖), where Walk 19 begins. This 9th-century settlement is a treasure-trove of old and restored buildings (see page 90 for picnic suggestions).

Returning to the D151, head left and, at the junction 500m along, turn right (D71 for CATERI/CALVI). **Cateri** (144km ✝✕) is one of my favourite villages. Pass above the Couvent de Marcasso on your right (where Walk 18 begins) and, on meeting the N197, turn left. Alternative walk 18 is based on **Lumio** ★ (151km ▲▲△✕🚌). You pass the road right to the Plage de l'Arinella, after which the first left turn leads to the 11th-century Romanesque San Pietro Church (✝), with its curious lion-headed portal. **Calvi** is straight on (161km).

Bastia • Macinaggio • Rogliano • Centuri-Port • Nonza • St-Florent • Patrimonio • Bastia

Roads on the east coast are good; those on the west are narrow and often bumpy. All are winding. Be on the alert for livestock on the roadside along the west coast. Reckon on 137km/85mi, 5h driving. Note that although I think this is the most attractive way to do this tour, drivers with nervous passengers might prefer to do the whole circuit in reverse, so that the car is always on the inland side of the roads.

En route: Walks 27, 28, 29, 33. Picnic suggestions for Walks 27 and 33 (both reached via bumpy tracks), but my favourite picnic spots on this tour are at Nonza (94.5km; see page 36).

Cap Corse stands apart from the rest of Corsica, both geographically and scenically. Contrasting coastal landscapes accompany you all the way on this tour: the east is gentle and subdued; the west sharp and dramatic. Watchtowers litter the countryside, and monasteries are as common as churches. Vestiges of the past lie around every corner. Small coves, some sandy, some pebbly, will draw you down to the magnetic turquoise sea. This excursion can be split into a leisurely two-day outing, the east coast one day, the west another.

Heading north on the D80 past **Pietranera** (3km 🏖️✕🏨) and **Miomo** (5.5km 🅿️🏖️△✕), you're still in residential confines. Posh villas in choice locations overlook the sea. Pass the turn-off left for Pozzo, starting point for the ascent of **Monte Stello★**, at 1307m/4285ft, the second-highest summit on the cape (Walk 29). **Lavasina** (⛪🏖️✕🏨) is the site of one of the island's most important festivals — the Nativity of the Virgin, celebrated on the 8th September. The 17th-century church, Notre Dame des Graces (with an unsightly campanile) houses a painting of the Virgin and Child which is revered by fishermen and attributed with miraculous powers. Walk 28, a short — but still pretty stiff! — hike, begins just by this church and climbs to the church at Pozzo, shown on page 108.

Before coming into **Erbalunga★** (10km 🅿️🏖️⛪✕), a favourite haunt of artists, you will spot it — a group of houses crammed onto a low spit of rock, sitting out in the water. The houses appear to 'grow' out of the sea. You can wander through the alleys of this curious old fishing village in five minutes. Four kilometres beyond Erbalunga, a balcony viewpoint (📷) juts out of the hillside below the road. A tiny, rather special rocky cove sits out of sight to the right of it. It's an ideal swimming spot.

If you can chase up the key for the parish Church of St-Martin up in the Commune de Sisco (enquire in advance at the tourist office in Bastia), you may like to look over its hoard of treasures: the bit of soil from which God made Adam, hairs from the cloak of St John the Baptist, and a fragment of a coat worn by the Virgin Mary … to mention but a few. The turn-off for Sisco

(D32) is at **Marine de Sisco** (15.5km 🏖△✖), from where the road rises for 7km through a lush tree-rich landscape, where hamlets of stone-built houses huddle in the shade. Once in **Sisco**, you'll have another search for the key to the simple, ideally-sited Romanesque San Michele Chapel (☨), not far above St-Martin (☨). To get there, turn right past St-Martin and after 500m turn left, up a rough narrow track. When you come to another fork, park and walk up to the right. Where the track swings left, continue along an overgrown path. When you come to the remains of a stone building, turn right along a hillside shelf and, 15 minutes from the car, you're there. Don't worry if you forgot the key; you have really climbed here for the views over the valley and across the sea to the islands off Tuscany.

Return to the coastal road and turn left.* The countryside loses its trees; the turquoise blue of the sea deepens. **Marine de Pietracorbara** (20km ⌂🏖✖), a pleasant resort of white sand set back in a U in the coast, boasts the first substantial beach you reach. The well-preserved Tour de l'Osse (⌂) serves as a particularly striking landmark, further along the coast. A pretty pebbly cove lies just below it. **Porticciolo** (26km 🏖✖) is a small village overlooking the sea. A tiny marina and narrow beach shelter in its shallow bay.

Beyond **Santa Severa** (28km ⛰△✖🏕) the D80 continues past an unspoilt shingle beach, before reaching the spread-out seaside village of **Marine de Meria** (34km ⌂🏖). Some four

Ruined Genoese watchtower at Punta Mortella (Walk 33)

Santa Maria chapel and ruined tower (Walk 27, near Macinaggio)

kilometres further on lies the busy yachting harbour of **Macin-aggio** (38.5km △△✕ ⚐). It sits at the end of a long sandy beach, which is excellent for children. Access to Walk 27 begins on the road to the right, opposite the post office (small sign, 'Plages de Tamarone').

Continuing west, leave the D80 some 4km beyond Macin-aggio: turn left (D53) for the historic **Commune de Rogliano**★ (▲▲). This settlement of eight hamlets dominates the surrounding hills with its many prominent buildings, arousing your curiosity long before you reach it. In **Bettolacce** (44.5km ⊟♀▲▲✕⬜) you come face to face with the Eglise St-Agnel, set high on the hillside, from where there is a superb view down over Macinaggio and the setting for Walk 27. Below the church sits the Chapel of the Confrérie de Ste-Croix and below that, the impressive Tour Franceschi, standing guard. Return from the tower to the D53 and go right for RD80, MACINAGGIO, remembering to look back at the scattering of mottled-grey houses ensconced amongst the trees. The ruins of the Convent of St Francis (♀) are glimpsed on a hilltop above, and the view over Macinaggio's bay is superb.

Turn left on the D80, to look straight off the end of the cape to the sharp islet of la Giraglia. Winding around scrub-covered hills, you pass the Tollare/Barcaggio junction (possible 15.5km detour on a bumpy road to the curving sandy beach of Barcaggio (▲▲✕; visited on the long version of Walk 27). The main tour keeps to the D80, climbing to the **Col de la Serra** (⬜). You could stretch your legs here by walking up to the **Moulin Mattei**★, an excellent viewpoint over the cape.

Centuri-Port, where you could have a lobster lunch instead of a picnic!

Once over the pass, the more dramatic western coast unfolds before you (📷). Sheer hills rise straight up out of the sea. Villages nestle on protruding ridges. Turn off *sharp right* on the D35 at **Camera** at a sign for PORT DE CENTURI (50km), squeezing through the hamlet. Soon a medieval-style château is passed (■), set amidst trees in a garden below the road. This 19th-century building belonged to General Cipriani. Head left at the fork beyond the château and wind down through olive trees and evergreen oaks. Keep to the D35 until you come to the parking area overlooking the scrub-covered Ilôt de Centuri. Then walk back into **Centuri-Port**★ (54.5km 🏖△✕) — definitely worth a stop. Lobsters are the speciality of the local fishermen, so if you feel like splurging, now is the time. The Sentier des Douaniers (see Walk 27) ends here.

From Centuri-Port, remain on the D35, heading south. Some large rotund watch-towers dot the hills. Rejoining the D80 (59km), you continue south around the seaside slopes. Shortly, a stunning bay, the **Aliso Gulf**, shines up at you. The grey collar of rock intensifies the contrast of forest-green vegetation and a crystalline blue sea. A steep rough track goes down to the beach, but it's best reached on foot. Notice the fascinating family mausoleums on this road, as you approach Pino.*

*Should you wish to make a detour to the Genoese Tour de Sénèque★ shown overleaf, turn left just before Pino on the D180 signposted for LURI/BASTIA. At the **Col de Ste-Lucie** (📷), turn right up a side-road for 1km, and park in the grounds of a walkers' *gîte*. The path to the tower starts here; it's steep and very slippery when wet; allow 1h20min return (a climb/descent of 120m/400ft).

Pino (69km ♣▲✕☐🎥) is a gracious hillside village, its houses scattered amidst a profusion of trees: cypress, palms, planes, oaks and olives. Looking back from here, you see sheer coastal ridges toppling off into the sea. The Convent of St Francis (☐♣), more impressive when seen from above, perches on a rocky shore down to the right. (The road to it is just 1km beyond Pino.) While the old convent now houses a private school, there is an interesting fresco in the chapel and a Genoese tower in the grounds.

The coastline becomes more exciting as you continue towards St-Florent. The D80 hangs out over sea cliffs that drop away into the indigo depths. Strips of overgrown terracing step stretches of near-vertical slopes; prickly-pear cactus is in its element. You pass through an outburst of jagged ridges and then curve inland up the Furcone Valley. Below is the **Marine de Giottani**, another pretty cove set in white rock. It quickly opens up into an irresistibly dazzling little beach. Most people drive past it slowly and, a minute later, turn round and go back to it. High above the sea again, an enormous building (which at first glance you might mistake for an hotel) disrupts the seascape. It's an abandoned asbestos mine. If you can ignore this awesome sight, you will enjoy the tremendous view across the hilly coastline towards the central massif and the bumpy Désert des Agriates. Black sand beaches lie below you here, further intensifying another colour contrast: white rock and royal-blue sea.

Your approach to **Nonza★** (94.5km ☐♣▲✕🎥) is spectacular. Its captivating beach, a long wide band of pebbles made almost inaccessible by the sheer-sided hills that rise up out of it, spans out directly below you. The village is superbly sited, built into a rocky spur that leans out over the tail of the beach some 150m/500ft below. A tower, marking the site of a medieval fort, crowns the spur: this is an awe-inspiring perch and a delightful place to unpack the picnic basket. You have stupendous views down onto the beach and over the orange, lichen-covered slate roof-tops of the village, splashed with purple bougainvillaea. Nonza was the birthplace of Saint Julie, a martyr crucified by the Romans. A pilgrimage to the Fountain of St Julie and its altar is held each year on the 22nd of May. If you find the tower perch a little too precarious for lunch, this altar and the two gushing fountains make another lovely picnic spot: they are below the road, on the path to the beach (signposted on the wall on your right, at the parking area just as you come into the village). Nonza's 16th-century church, with a tableau depicting St Julie, is above the road, almost opposite the beach path.

Closer to St-Florent, you begin descending. The coastline

Left: the Genoese church of St-Martin rises above vineyards at Patrimonio. Right: the Tour de Sénèque

eases out and is less exciting visually. Some vineyards and orchards soothe the approach. Five kilometres before the town, at a roundabout where Bastia is signed to the left, take the first exit, the D81 for ST-FLORENT/L'ILE-ROUSSE. **St-Florent★** (114km ⬛♨⛰🏠△✕🍴⊕WC), where Walk 33 begins and ends, is an extremely pleasant resort. Set deep in the gulf, on the banks of the Alisio River, it clusters round a huge citadel that dominates the port. The Genoese part of the town (**Nebbio★**), however, sits 1km further inland. All that remains of it is the 12th-century cathedral church of Santa Maria Assunta, one of the island's masterpieces. (A sister edifice, La Canonica, may be visited during Tour 'Bastia 3'.) The key to this outstanding example of Romanesque architecture is obtainable (for a small deposit) from the tourist office on the Bastia road.

Retrace the D81 the 5km back to the Bastia roundabout and turn right for BASTIA. Just inside **Patrimonio** (121km ♨⛰✕), in front of the post office, turn left for the 16th-century Eglise St-Martin (♨). While the interior holds nothing of great interest, this elegant church, with its graceful steeple, is very photogenic. Patrimonio is known for its private (as opposed to co-operative) vineyards; quality, not quantity, is the vintners' aim. You can sample reds, whites, rosés and muscatels.

The **Col de Teghime★** (📷) is the pass that breaches the high hills separating St-Florent from Bastia. From here there is a grand panorama over the eastern and western side of the cape and, on hazeless days, towards Elba. Finer still are the views from the **Serra di Pigno★** (📷): the signposted turn-off (D338) is on the left, not far over the pass; the viewpoint is 4km uphill.

Return to the D81 and descend to **Bastia** (137km).

Bastia • Ponte Leccia • Corte • Gorges de la Restonica • (Murato • Défilé de Lancone) • Bastia

*The road to Corte is good, but the single-lane road in the Restonica Valley is very precipitous, and there are no barriers. Note that vehicles **descending** this road have right of way (in case of brake failure). Note also that there is a restriction on the size of vehicle that can use this road (some camper vans are considered too wide), and that not all mopeds can handle the steep ascent. The detour route from Ponte Nuovo to Murato and the Défilé de Lancone is equally precipitous. These narrow roads may be closed in early spring and late autumn. Even if they are open, they are not recommended in bad weather: rock fall is common, and it can be very cold. Watch out for foraging animals. Reckon on 169km/105mi, 6h driving if you return via your outgoing route; add 34km/21mi, 1h30min if you return by the 'detour route'.*

En route: Walks 30, 31, 32; picnic suggestions for Walks 31 and 32. Walks 4-9, lovely excursions around Venaco and Vizzavona, each with a picnic suggestion, are easily reached from Corte.

W ho needs beaches when there are rivers as beautiful as the Restonica? This breathtaking gorge merits a full day out — and *don't miss* the lakes visited on Walk 31. Young belles struggle up to them in high heels, and babies go up on dad's back; everyone climbs to see the magnetic beauty of these mirror-like lakes. And when the day is ending, you can throw yourselves into one of the many delicious pools that fill the valley floor.

The tour follows the N193 from Bastia all the way to Corte. At **Casamozza** (20km 🏠🏔✕🅿) you leave the coastal plains behind and come into the Golo Valley, a hilly unkempt area with small farm plots stretching across the narrow river flats. Danger signs warn against swimming in the river; they are there for a good reason! At **Ponte Nuovo** (38km 🅿) you pass the D5 to Murato, an optional detour for the homeward leg. The valley opens up: orchards, vineyards and hayfields cover the floor. Pass through **Ponte Leccia** (46km 🏠🏔△✕🅿), the crossroads of the north, and follow the Golo River.

A tunnel takes you under the San Quilico Pass: you leave the Golo and descend towards Corte. The countryside is pastoral and clear of maquis, with straw-coloured hills. Approaching the town, turn off right for *CORTE CENTRE* on the D2193. Cross the Orla River, then continue south on the main street through **Corte ★** (70km 🏛👥🏠🏔 △✕🅿⊕🗺MWC), past plain but pleasant tall buildings. Set at the confluence of the Tavignano and Restonica rivers, in the shadow of the central massif, this is Corsica's university town — quite unaffected by tourism. The old quarter terraces a steep hillface, and a 15th-century fortress crowns the citadel. Corte is a fine base for walks and drives into the central mountains, around Venaco and Vizzavona.

The turn-off for Walk 30 is on the south side of town, just *before* the Tavignano (signed 'CITADELLE'). Just *over* the river is

The 12th-century Pisan Romanesque church of San Michele di Murato rises in splendid isolation on a flat crest (detour route on the return to Bastia).

the road to **La Restonica★**. Turn right on the D623 and head up alongside the bounding crystal-clear river (▲▲ ✕). Watch out for cows in the middle of the road! Climbing rapidly, you enter pines. Below the road, small inviting river flats, cushioned in grass and ferns and shaded by pines, make splendid picnic spots. Coming into alpine pastures, the pines subside and only a few grand species remain. Not far beyond the Pont de Grotelle (starting point for Walk 32), the road ends at the enchanting **Bergeries de Grotelle** (84.5km), a settlement of low stone houses and animal pens. If you're walking up to the lakes (see photographs pages 114 and 116), park here.

In hot weather you may want to end the excursion with a dip in one of those inviting pools further downstream, before returning the same way to **Bastia** (169km).

Detour: But if it's too cold or you would rather be driving, then take this long route back. Just over the bridge at Ponte Nuovo, turn left on the D5 for LENTO. This ascent, on a very narrow road, affords views back down the Golo. Pass through **Lento**, a village set back on tree-patched slopes. As you enter **Bigorno**, the D5 hairpins up left to a pass, the **Bocca di Bigorno★** (📷), from where there are fine views over the Golo to table-topped Monte San Petrone above the hills of la Castagniccia and Monte Sant' Angelu above Loreto. Over the pass, a rolling plateau stretches before you; then you descend through hills laced with chestnut groves. Beyond **Murato** (✕🍴), you soon spot the church of San Michele (⚓) on a flat crest ahead to the right. From here you look down onto the Aliso basin, and the Gulf of St-Florent fills in the backdrop. Descending to a roundabout, take the second exit (D62), into the **Défilé de Lancone★**. You'll get only a glimpse of the gorge on this hair-raising road where everyone hoots with anxiety as they round each bend. But a superb view over the green-embroidered plains of Bastia and the Biguglia Lagoon greets you just before you leave the gorge. Turn left on the N193 to **Bastia** (203km).

Bastia • Ponte Leccia • Morosaglia • la Porta • Piedicroce • Cervione • San Nicolao • Bastia

Some of the country roads followed on this tour are narrow and winding. Watch out for foraging livestock. There are no petrol stations between Ponte Leccia and Cervione (85km). Reckon on 172km/107mi, 5h30min driving.

En route: Walk 34 (with picnic suggestion). There is another recommended picnic spot just before San Nicolao (127km).

There are no real 'sights' on this tour; it is simply a most enjoyable day's outing in a landscape bumpy with hills and thick with the chestnut groves that give their name to the region, the Castagniccia. Small rustic villages echo the silence, with their shuttered houses and boarded-up churches. A pleasant surprise along the way: the old roadside fountains have been restored, given names, and gush forth water once again.

Follow Tour 'Bastia 2' to **Ponte Leccia** (46km). Just before crossing the Golo, turn left on the D71 for MOROSAGLIA. Climbing amidst low abrupt hills, you overlook the Golo Valley. The Aig de Popolasca, a high craggy mass, rears up above the far valley wall. Further along to the left the great Rotondo massif is seen. Junipers and pines share the lower slopes; higher up, cork trees stand out with their crusty bark. (You'll often see a large square piece neatly cut out of the trunk. These trees can only be stripped when 25 years old — and then only once every 10-12 years.)

Travelling east, you skirt the upper Golo Valley and look out over the hills above Ponte Nuovo (the 'detour route' in Car tour 'Bastia 2'). **Morosaglia** (60.5km ✝M) has a claim to fame: Pasquale Paoli, Corsica's great patriot, was born here. His birthplace is a museum (open daily 09.00-12.00; 15.00-18.00). The Romanesque church of Santa Reparata, where he was baptised, sits above the village; his school (the present village school and named for him) is the grand building on the right as you enter the village. It was formerly the Rostino Monastery and a meeting place for members of the Corsican Liberation Movement in the early 18th century. This pretty village lies scattered deep in the hills amidst chestnut groves. The name of the region, **la Castagniccia ★**, derives from the Latin word for sweet chestnut — once the mainstay of the local people. Not only was the flour an important part of their diet and the wood used for furniture, farm tools and fuel, but both were bartered for goods from other regions.

Beyond Morosaglia, you come to the Col de Prato (📷), where you can park for Walk 34. Now the sea reappears in the distance over the hills. The rugged inland Fium' Altu, a valley of ridges and hills saturated in trees, stretches out before you. Hamlets lie sporadically dispersed across the inclines. Not far below the pass (some 5km from Morosaglia), turn *sharp left* on a narrow road that swings downhill towards STOPPIA/LA PORTA. This lovely road (D205) twirls its way round the hillsides under an arcade of trees. The countryside is crisp with arboreal greenery. You squeeze through and then past a couple of old grey hamlets. Just after you join a road coming from the left, **la Porta★** (72km ✝🏔✖) comes into sight, adorning the crest of a declining ridge. The church campanile immediately steals your attention. This elegant, oriental-looking bell tower is supposedly the finest baroque tower on the island but, once alongside it, you discover that the 1720 structure has suffered a rather heavy-handed facelift. Park in the square and visit the church however: it's so seldom that one finds a church open on this island! The interior of St-Jean-Baptiste is lavishly decorated, with a beautifully-painted organ loft. Time for morning coffee? Find the *boulangérie*, buy some custard tarts and head over to the café. Then continue on through **Croce** (78km **M** of local customs, open Sat/Sun afternoons only). **Monte San Petrone★** (1767m/5795ft; photograph page 122), the goal of Walk 34, is the most prominent upthrust in the area, with its rocky crest.

Return to the D71 and turn left. This is the route of the drinking fountains: many are lovingly restored, and all are different. Art enthusiasts may like to summon up the energy to locate the key for the Church of St André in **Campana** (83km ✝) and then climb up to it. It holds a painting attributed to Zubarán or one of his pupils. Here Monte San Petrone rises up just beside you.

The Orezza Monastery (✝) is the impressive skeleton of a building you pass further on, draped in creepers. Once a seat for the Corsican Liberation Movement, this is where Paoli was elected Commander-in-Chief of the Corsican National Guard. It was destroyed in 1943. Further along you enter **Piedicroce** (87km ✝🏔✖) and pass the massive church of St Peter and St Paul, with a 17th-century organ said to be the oldest on Corsica and a 16th-century painting on wood of the Virgin and Child. Entering **Carcheto-Brustico★** (90.5km ✝), a narrow lane off left descends to the church of St Margaret, where (if you can find the key) you would see two works of local origin, an alabaster statuette and a painting of the Stations of the Cross in a Corsican setting.

The **Bocca d'Arcarota** (✖🏞) opens your way to the vast Alesani Valley, flooded with trees. The sinuous road describes a deep V, where the cloak of deciduous trees fades out, and a tangle of maquis takes over. The twisting tail of the Alesani Dam later catches your eye in the valley floor, with its cloudy-green water (with unmarked 🖭). Continuing the descent, your view stretches all along the undulating sea plain. **Cervione** (121km ✝🔺✕🏠M 🖭) is a balcony village, hooded by chestnuts and olive trees. The imposing church here, St Mary and St Erasmus, dwarfs even the tall houses that surround it. The Bishop's Palace (noticeably renovated) houses a museum of local archaeology (open daily except Sun/hol: 10.00-12.00; 14.30-18.00). Just beyond Cervione you come into **Valle-di-Campoloro**. Here you could ask at the *mairie*/school for the key to the chapel of Santa Cristina ★ (✝): the turn-off is 0.5km past the village sign (just beyond the *mairie*), a sharp turn back down to the left indicated by a small brown sign. Fork left again 1km down this country lane, onto a dirt track signposted 'SANTA MARIA'. (Better still, walk; the track is very bumpy.) The chapel holds exquisite 15th-century frescoes: the pastel colours are still sharp, the facial expressions still very clearly defined.

From here return to the San Nicolao junction in Valle-di-Campoloro (D330) and turn right. Beyond a tunnel you look straight up into a couple of small waterfalls that leap down from a gap in the hillside. A path from the lay-by just past here would take you to them — an ideal picnic spot, with a shallow pool. Arriving at **San Nicolao** (127km ✝🔺✕), a shady hillside village, you come to an intersection (🖭) with a fine view over a solitary 17th-century baroque church with a six-storied campanile (✝). Head right on the D34 and, at the N198 turn left, back to **Bastia** (172km). (Or fit in this detour: take the airport exit, then turn right immediately on the D107, to visit La Canonica (✝), one of Corsica's finest churches (Romanesque, 12c). The ancient city of Mariana was founded here in 93BC. The 11th-century church of San Parteo (✝) is nearby. Continue to Bastia via the pretty lagoon.)

Cervione: the buildings are dwarfed by the church of St Mary and St Erasmus.

Porto-Vecchio: THE OSPEDALE AND BAVELLA MASSIFS, AND A SUNSET OVER BONIFACIO

Porto-Vecchio • l'Ospédale • Zonza • Col de Bavella • Solenzara • Pinarellu • San Ciprianu • Plage de Palombaggia • Bonifacio • Porto-Vecchio

The roads are generally good but very winding. In bad weather the first part of the tour (as far as Solenzara) is not recommended, due to poor visibility and the possibility of rockfall. Always be alert for foraging livestock. The high passes can be very cold, with gale-force winds. Reckon on 217km/135mi; about 7h driving.

En route: Walks 35, 36, 37, 38, 39, 40 (all with good picnic spots)

Ideally this drive should be a leisurely two-day affair, so that you can fit in several short, very spectacular walks, through some of the island's most impressive pink-granite mountains. But if you can't wait until tomorrow, make a mad dash to Bonifacio, to watch the sun set over the island's most dramatic town.

Setting out on the D368 from Porto-Vecchio, head towards Zonza, through countryside lightly wooded in the cork trees for which this region is well known. Their stripped trunks are a curious sight. A winding road leads you into the large sprawling hills on the spine of the Ospédale massif, which is home to a splendid forest of maritime pines. You enjoy stunning views over the deeply-etched Golfe de Porto-Vecchio and inland along the wide, open Stabiacco Valley that stretches back off the gulf. Bright green fields lining the valley floor stand out in this otherwise dark green countryside.

L'Ospédale (19km ✕🖼) takes its name from the hospital that was on this site in Roman times. It commands a magnificent panorama over the gulfs of Porto-Vecchio and Santa Manza. A small summer retreat, its granite-block houses sit well camouflaged high on the wooded hillside amidst great boulders of granite. Your first chance for a walk comes up just 1km outside l'Ospédale, where a road leads left to 'AGNARONE'. This may be too far off your route during this long car tour (see map at the bottom of page 130), but Walk 39 *is a must* at some point during your time in the south, especially if you visit in spring.

Continuing on the D368, you wind through the forest. Huge mounds of rock grow out of the cover of trees. You skirt the **Barrage de l'Ospédale★** (🖼), a glimmering reservoir that lies at the foot of Punta di Corbu. Some 3.5km past the dam wall, cars galore and a kiosk alert you to the large parking area on the right for Walk 37 to the **Cascade de Piscia di Gallo★**, illustrated on page 128). A third chance to stretch your legs comes up at the **Bocca d'Illarata** (991m/3250ft), where the ascent of Monte Calva begins (Walk 38). But it's the many facets of the Punta di u Diamanti just off the road that catch the eye (photograph page 129).

Over the pass you descend through forest (△) into **Zonza**

43

(40.5km ⛰✖�). Chestnut trees announce the beginning of this village. It sits at crossroads, deep in the hills. Here turn right on the D268 and climb to the **Col de Bavella**★ (1218m/ 4000ft; 49km 📷) — one of Corsica's most breathtaking viewpoints. The impenetrable valley walls, with their needle-sharp crags (the 'Aiguilles de Bavella') can be anything from a deep red to a soft rose colour. Seeing is believing! Large windswept pines stand here on the pass, as does a statue to Our

The Barrage de l'Ospédale, at the foot of Punta di Corbu

Lady of the Snows. The hamlet of **Bavella** (⚫✕) huddles just over the pass. A small gathering of stone, wood and corrugated iron dwellings, it is more like a pastoral outpost than a hamlet. Walks 35 and 36 begin opposite the inn (photographs pages 124 and 126).

You descend in hairpin bends through a valley dominated by towering granite walls. Notice the flat-topped pines: this is not the latest fashion in tree trimming; the strong winds are to blame. On the lower inclines you wend your way through plantations of firs, young pines, and chestnut trees. Closer to the valley floor, keep an eye open for a rocky outcrop that resembles a sitting dog (a terrier?). It's on a ridge on your left, about 15km downhill.

Once on the valley floor, you're in the company of the Solenzara River, a wide bouldery river bordered by beach-like stretches of sand. River swimmers will want to take a dip in its inviting pools, which are suitable for children. When you meet the N198, turn right to pass through the sea-side town of **Solenzara** (80km ⛰️△✕ ⬛⊕) and follow the coast back towards Porto-Vecchio. This stretch of coastline is flat and rocky, with a few pleasant beaches collaring the small bays. You pass behind the sweeping beaches of **Favone** (92km ⛰️⚫△✕) and **Tarco** (96km ⛰️⚫△✕). Curving round into an open bay, you spot a Genoese tower on a promontory, the **Punta di Fautea** (100km ⬛△✕).

Turning inland, the N198 soon enters **Ste-Lucie-de- Porto-Vecchio** (105km ⛰️✕⬛). Branch off left here onto the D168a, to see some of Porto-Vecchio's best-known beaches. Outside high season, **Pinarellu** (108km ⬛⛰️⚫ △✕⬛) is a quiet, unassuming resort, sitting in a deep bay and guarded by a Genoese tower set on a tiny islet. It boasts a fine beach bordered with pines. A pretty rural drive over a sometimes narrow and bumpy road leads you along the D468 to the next resort: some 8km from Pinarellu, at the roundabout, take the third exit (D668). After 1km you come to a sweeping sandy beach at **San Ciprianu** (118km ⛰️△✕⬛). If these first two beaches didn't take your fancy however, then try the next turn off to the left, the D468a, to the fine beach at **Cala Rossa** (⛰️⚫△✕).

Continuing along the D468, you pass behind ritzy **Golfo di Sogno** (⛰️✕), which also offers good swimming in its sheltered bay. Further on, you're distracted by the prominent chain of inland mountains and the bay, with the fortified town of Porto-Vecchio on the far side. Rejoining the N198, decide whether to call it a day or make for Bonifacio.

At the roundabout you encounter just outside Porto-Vecchio (128km) keep right for BONIFACIO, to bypass the centre. At the seventh roundabout, take the third exit for PALOMBAGGIA, to see the island's most highly-rated beach. Circling the Stabiacco estuary, you look across the reedy tidal river with its pine-studded sand banks, to Porto-Vecchio (☎). A small pass takes you over the hills to **Piccovagia**.

Detour: From Piccovagia you could make a detour to the **Pointe de la Chiappa** (☎; add 6km return). If so, take the first left turn; there may be a sign here, 'PHARE'. Follow this narrow tarred lane where it ends at the top of a crest between two lighthouses (military and civilian), with an impressive view over the bays of San Ciprianu and Stagnolo and onto the mountainous backdrop. On the left side of the point lie some rocky islets, the Iles Cerbicale.

The main tour continues straight through Piccovagia; after 1.5km, fork left for the **Plage de Palombaggia★** (150km ⛰⛰▲△✕). This long unspoilt beach with its crystal-clear water, red rock, and low sand dunes is shaded by beautiful umbrella-shaped parasol pines. It would be easy just to lose the rest of the day here.

Return to the junction for the beach and turn left. More of this vast beach reveals itself through the trees along the shore. Sadly, the buildings do little to help conserve this very special stretch of coastline. At the village of **Bocca dell' Oro** (160km ✕) keep right to rejoin the N198, where you turn left for BONIFACIO. Heading through low hills wooded in cork trees and maquis, you eventually join the N196 at a roundabout and come into **Bonifacio★** (187km ⛽⛰⛰▲△✕🅿WC☎). The most convenient car park is on the left on entering the harbour complex but out of season you should be able to find a place higher up. To visit the citadel and old town, keep heading uphill past the port (Avenue Charles de Gaulle). This magnificently sited town overhangs the sea from its cliff-top perch. Set on a high, narrow headland, Bonifacio enjoys superb sea views on both sides. To the south it looks along the dramatic, glaring-white sea cliffs, to the north down into the fjord-like inlet, and inland to the Cagna hills. Walk around the old town, inside the imposing citadel walls. The elegant old buildings that line the narrow and shady streets are treasures of history. The Eglise Sainte-Marie-Majeure was built by both the Pisans (in the late 12th century) and the Genoese; its tall campanile dates from the 14th and 15th centuries. The relics of St Boniface, the town's patron saint, are kept here, as is a piece of the 'True Cross'. Other churches of interest are St-François (1390) and St-Dominique, a Gothic church started in 1270 by the Knights Templar and finished by the Dominicans in 1343. The pillars of this latter church (between the aisles and the nave) have small paintings

Seascapes on Walk 40 from Bonifacio (see also photo page 133)

dating from the 18th century, representing the Fifteen Mysteries of the Rosary.

If you're spending the day at Bonifacio, among the more popular beaches are Calalonga, Rondinara, and those in the Golfe de Santa-Manza. Or you may want to take one of the boat trips on offer ... perhaps to the small granite Iles de Lavezzi, which boast a variety of unusual flora. Another popular excursion is to the sea caves, where you can see the famous 'King of Aragon's Staircase' with its 187 steps. Sardinia is also easily accessible from here.

If you want to keep driving, visit the **Ermitage de la Trinité ★** (⚓), 7km west of Bonifacio: head west towards Sartène and take the first left turn off the N196. This ancient sanctuary is the sight of a local pilgrimage, but it's best known for its striking view back onto Bonifacio. Finally, don't miss Walk 40. Of course you *can* explore **Capo Pertusato ★** by car, but the road is closed beyond the semaphore; the lighthouse at the end of the cape is only accessible on foot. And you miss most of the dramatic coastline if you drive. Sunset is a fine time to end Walk 40, when the cliffs are aglow.

From Bonifacio take the N198 straight back to **Porto-Vecchio** (217km).

☀ *Walking*

This book describes some 70 long and short walks, chosen for their accessibility from the centres most popular with holiday-makers and covering a good cross-section of the island's varied landscapes. Corsica is a walkers' paradise. The grants the island has received from the EU have been mostly spent on protecting the environment and developing new walks.

There are various local walks ('Sentiers de Pays'), based on centres like Venaco. Private land abutting the sea has been purchased to create miles of coastal paths, and the Office National des Forêts has developed woodland nature trails. The Parc Régional de la Corse has established six excellent long-distance trails. Of these, the best known is the GR20. Less strenuous routes are two 'Mare e Monti' ('Sea and Mountains') footpaths, one in the north and another in the south, and three 'Mare a Mare' ('Sea to Sea') paths — in the north, centre and south. All are well waymarked and dotted with refuges.

Several of these trails are followed in part during walks in this book. But as with all 'Landscapes' guides, all the walks can be completed in a day's outing from your overnight base, and almost all can be reached by public transport.

G rading, waymarking, maps, GPS
We've tried to give you a quick overview of each walk's **grade** in the Contents, but there is only space to show the *lowest* grade of a *main* walk: for full details, including easier versions, see the walk itself. Here is a brief overview of the four gradings:

● very easy — more or less level (perhaps with a short climb to a viewpoint); good surfaces underfoot; easily followed

● easy-moderate — ascents/descents of no more than about 300-500m/1000-1800ft; good surfaces underfoot; easily followed

● moderate-strenuous — ascents/descents may be over 500m/1800ft; variable surfaces underfoot — you must be sure-footed and agile; possible route-finding problems in poor visibility

● expert — only suitable for very experienced hillwalkers

Any of the above grades may be followed by:

⁝ *danger* of vertigo for those with no head for heights

Waymarking is consistent on the GR20 (red/white flashes) and the 'Mare e Monti' and 'Mare a Mare' trails (orange flashes). But local walks use various colours *(which can change from year to year)*, signposts ... or nothing at all. Nature trails are often marked with wooden posts.

The **maps** in this book (scale 1:50,000) should be sufficient for all the walks described. They are based on IGN 'Top 25' (1:25,000) maps and our GPS work in the field. Should you wish to go further afield, IGN maps are available everywhere on Corsica, and the number of the relevant sheet is shown at the beginning of each walk, under 'Equipment'.

Free **GPS track** downloads are available for all these walks: see the *Landscapes of Corsica* page on the Sunflower website and click on the 'GPS' tab. Please bear in mind, however, that GPS readings should *never* be relied upon as your sole reference point, as conditions can change overnight. *But even if you don't use GPS,* it's great fun opening our GPX files in Google Earth to preview the walks in advance!

Where to stay
The walks have been written up from four bases: **Ajaccio/Porto, Calvi, Bastia** and **Porto-Vecchio**. Not only are these the most popular tourist areas, but they are also quite well served by public transport. (GPS coordinates are given for the start of each walk, so that motorists can set their satnavs.)

The independent traveller will find **hotels**, **apartments**, *pensions* and **campsites** in most corners of the island. However, many are only open from June 15th to September 15th. *Note:* In July and August nearly all the accommodation is booked — some of it months in advance. During June and September, reserving a couple of days in advance is usually sufficient, but not in the peak months! The rates for accommodation outside July and August are also far more reasonable than in high season. Never be afraid to ask for a discount out of season.

Gîtes (country cottages) are also widely scattered across the island. These are usually rented by the week or month. *Gîtes d'étape* are inns geared for long-distance walkers and cyclists, with shared rooms. Meals are usually provided — and the cooking is often superb. For information (in English) see www.gites-corsica.co.uk.

Refuges are liberally dotted around the central mountains. Part of the GR20/Mare e Monti/Mare a Mare programme, they are well maintained, open all year round, and fully equipped (gas, kitchen utensils, beds, etc).

Language
English is not usually understood outside the principal tourist areas, but everyone speaks French. The local language (*lingua corsa*) is widely spoken (and now taught in all schools and colleges). If you speak Italian you will be understood, and to a certain degree understand the island dialect, since it is similar to peninsular Tuscan. Try to learn at least a few words of

greeting and thanks in the local language — your efforts will be greatly appreciated.

Corsican spellings are widely used for place names, but these may vary even when referring to the same place! You will spot inconsistencies in the text, on maps, and on local signposts; unfortunately, this is unavoidable.

Weather

Mid-June until mid-September is most reliable for walking on Corsica — and for swimming, too. On either side of this 'high season', the weather can be changeable, which means that some of the mountain walks can be extremely dangerous. Snow may lie as low as 1000m/ 3300ft in June and may fall again late in September.

In **May** and **October** you will usually encounter more good days than bad ones, but be sure of the weather before setting off for the mountains. Cloud or mist sometimes descends without warning, and the temperatures fall rapidly. May and October are best suited for walks below 1000m. The weather, even if it turns bad, is not usually bad enough to ruin an entire day, but it can get very cold. These are, however, the months of the flowers and autumnal colours. In spring the countryside is scented with the strong perfume of the maquis; in autumn the beech and chestnut groves are an extravaganza of yellows and golds, and the shepherds return with their flocks — a wonderful sight.

July and **August** are the really hot months, with temperatures in the 30s. Things to fear are dehydration, frightening electrical storms and forest fires. *Always carry plenty of water;* many mountain streams dry up in the summer. **Electrical storms** usually come with plenty of warning: *quickly* seek shelter away from exposed places.

As a general rule, the north of Corsica is hotter than the south, and the east is wetter than the west. And Ajaccio boasts the most sunshine in the whole of France.

Wind patterns on the island make for quite a study! Here are some names you might hear or see in the papers:

Libeccio: a strong wind from the southwest, hot and dry in summer; in winter it carries rain to the west;

Maestral: the Corsican version of the *mistral,* this wind comes from the northwest and is unpleasant all year round, with a whining violence. Fortunately, it blows infrequently;

Sirocco: a dry dusty wind from the southeast;

Grecale: blowing from the northeast, it carries rain to the north, but leaves the south unaffected;

Tramontane: a dry cold wind from the north, it blows very infrequently, but is strong enough to knock you off your feet;

Mezzogiorno: the 'midday' wind, caused by the interaction of the hot sun and the still-cold sea; it raises strong sea breezes along the coast.

Most bars and cafés have the local newspaper *(Corse Matin)* available, with **diagrammatic weather maps**.

What to take

If you've come to Corsica without any special equipment such as a rucksack or walking boots, you can still do many of the walks — or you can buy the basic equipment on the island. *Don't* attempt the more difficult walks without the proper gear. For each walk in the book, the *minimum* year-round equipment is listed. Above all, you need stout, thick-soled shoes or walking boots. *Ankle support* is always advisable and is *essential* on some of the walks, where the path descends steeply over loose stones. You may find the following checklist useful:

At the top of each walk I recommend only the *special* equipment you might need; use the list below as a reminder, and go equipped according to the terrain and the season. *Always carry ample sun protection and plenty of water, and* **always be fully equipped for all extremes of weather**. Every year deaths are reported, and these are almost invariably caused through lack of caution.

stout shoes with ankle support or walking boots	bathing things	tissues
	small rucksack	insect repellent
	telescopic walking stick(s)	antiseptic cream
waterproof rain gear (outside summer)	sunhat, sunglasses, suncream	water bottle, plastic plates, etc
long trousers, tight at the ankles	knives and openers	first aid kit, with bandages and plasters
long-sleeved shirt (sun protection)	whistle	'Dog Dazer' (see 'Things that bite ...', page 51)
lightweight fleece	torch	
extra pair of long socks	compass or GPS	mobile or smartphone (the EU-wide emergency number is 112)
windcheat, gloves	plastic groundsheet	
jacket or woollen shirt	up-to-date timetables spare bootlaces	

Things that bite, sting, or shoot

Dogs are not generally a problem on Corsica, since most of the time you'll be far from habitation. In summer, however, some of the shepherds' dogs may send shivers down your spine. Let the shepherd know you're around, and you won't have any worries. Lone country houses always have a guard dog … or three. Watch their tails and heed their barks and growls. If you're worried, you could invest in an ultrasonic 'Dog Dazer': these are widely available on the web.

The **shooting season** for all game is from the third Sunday in August until the first Sunday in January. Some bird-shooting extends until the end of March. It can be very unnerving to have hunters blasting away all around you! If you fear they are too close, don't be afraid to bellow out — in *any* language!

You'll be pleased to read that while **snakes** and **insects** are to be found on the island, none has a fatal bite or sting.

A country code for walkers and motorists

The experienced rambler is used to following a 'country code', but the tourist out for a lark may unwittingly cause damage, harm animals, and even endanger his own life. Do heed this advice:

- *Lighting fires is forbidden. Corsica is prone to summer forest fires; do all you can to keep the island green and beautiful.*
- **Do not frighten animals.** The livestock you will encounter when touring and walking are not tame. By making loud noises or trying to touch or photograph them, you may cause them to run in fear and be hurt.
- **Walk quietly** through all farms, hamlets and villages, **leaving all gates just as you found them.**
- **Protect all wild and cultivated plants.** Don't try to pick wild flowers or uproot saplings. Obviously fruit and crops are someone's private property and should not be touched. *Never walk over cultivated land.*
- **Take all your litter away with you.**
  The following points cannot be stressed too strongly:
  — **Do not take risks.** Do not attempt walks beyond your capacity and **never walk alone**. Four people make the best walking group: in case of injury, someone can stay with the injured person, while two go for help. Always tell a responsible person *exactly* where you are going and what time you plan to return: if your party is lost or one of your group is injured, rescue services would be notified that much more quickly.
  — **At any time a walk may become unsafe** due to fire or storm damage, or the havoc caused by bulldozers. If the route is not as described in this book, and your way ahead is not secure, do *not* attempt to continue.
  — **Strenuous walks** are unsuitable in high summer.
  — **Mountain walks** are unsuitable in wet weather.
  — **Do not overestimate your energy**: your speed will be determined by the slowest walker in the group.
  — **Transport** at the end of the walk may be vital.
  — **Proper shoes or boots** are a necessity.
  — **Warm clothing** is needed in the mountains; even in summer, take something appropriate with you, in case you are delayed or injured.
  — **Extra food and drink** should be taken on long walks.
  — **Always take a sunhat**; cover arms and legs as well on sunny days.

Organisation of the walks

The 40 main walks in this book are grouped in four sections, chiefly for the ease of those travelling by public transport (or hiring a taxi): Ajaccio/Porto (Walks 1-15), Calvi (Walks 16-26), Bastia (Walks 27-34) and Porto-Vecchio (Walks 35-40). If you have a car, naturally a far greater range of rambles will be within easy reach.

I hope that the book is set out so that you can plan your walks easily — depending on how far you want to go, your abilities and equipment ... and what time you are willing to get up in the morning! You might begin by considering the fold-out touring map inside the back cover. Here you can see at a glance the overall terrain, the road and rail network, and the location of all the walks.

Quickly flipping through the book, you'll find that there is at least one photograph for every walk. Having selected one or two potential excursions from the map and the photographs, look over the planning information at the beginning of the walks. Here you'll find distance/walking time, grade, equipment, how to get there by public transport, and where to park if you are travelling by car. If the walk appears to be beyond your fitness or ability, check to see if a short or alternative version is described, which *would* appeal to you. On very hot days, the Short walks and Picnic suggestions may be as strenuous an adventure as you'd like to tackle.

When you are on your walk, you will find that the text begins with an introduction to the overall landscape and then quickly turns to a detailed description of the route itself. The large-scale walking maps (all scale 1:50,000) have been specially annotated to show key landmarks and, where possible, set out facing the walking notes. Times are given for reaching certain points in the walk. I have tried to estimate these times for the average, reasonably fit walker. As a rule of thumb, reckon on 4km/h on a good track on the flat and add one hour for every 300m/1000ft of ascent. *No time is included for stops;* increase the times by *at least* 50% to allow for lunch stops, photography and the like.

Finally, before travelling, be sure to log on to the Sunflower website and the 'Updates' tab on the *Landscapes of Corsica* page, to see if we have received any news since the book was published.

Below is a **key to the symbols** on the walking maps:

primary road		car parking.bus stop
secondary road		railway station.waypoint
minor road		spring, fountain, waterfall
motorable or other track		water tank, reservoir
cart track		*P* recommended picnic spot
footpath		best views.picnic tables
walking route and direction		building.campsite
alternative route		transmitter.quarry
— 150 — height (m)		helicopter landing pad
church.cross.cemetery		railway.railway tunnel
castle or fort.ancient site		sports ground
mill.windmill.watchtower		danger of vertigo!

Walk 1: POINTE DE LA PARATA • ANSE DE MINACCIA • POINTE DE LA PARATA

Distance/time: 13.5km/8.4mi; 3h05min

Grade: ● easy, but quite long, and with some thorny scrub on route. *No shade on beaches, nor any waymarking.* Overall ascents/descents of 150m/490ft

Equipment: as page 50; light shoes, sun protection, bathing things and plenty of water recommended; *IGN map 4153 OT*

Access: 🚗 or 🚌 (Timetable 1) to/from the large car park at the Pointe de la Parata (41° 54.109'N, 8° 37.108'E)

Alternative walks

1 Pointe de la Parata — Capigliolo — D111 (11km/6.8mi; 2h45min; ● grade as main walk, but with overall ascents and descents of 280m/920ft). Access by bus as above. Follow the main walk to the Anse de Minaccia. Then return to Capigliolo, climb the motorable track up to the D111b (**❺**), and turn right downhill to the D111 (**❻**; bus stop).

2 Sentier des Crêtes: ● A well-signposted walk, the Sentier des Crêtes, runs from the Bois des Anglais near the centre of Ajaccio out towards the Pointe de la Parata. But I prefer to pick it up out on the point and walk back to town. Gluttons for punishment might like to tack it onto Alternative walk 1, but it makes a good hike in its own right. It's about 10.5km/6.5mi from **❻** (the bus stop at the end of Alternative walk 1) to Ajaccio, with a gradual height gain of about 400m/1300ft and takes about three hours. It is not all shown on our map, but the signposted start at **❼** *is* shown — and a GPS track is available to download. If you decide to call it a day before you get all the way into Ajaccio, there are three opportunities to drop down from the trail to the D111 for a bus, all of them signposted. If you start in Ajaccio, take 🚌 Line 7 to the Bois des Anglais; if you start near La Parata, take Line 5 (Timetable 1) or Line 7 when you get back to town.

The Genoese Tour de la Parata (top), with the Iles Sanguinaires stretching out behind it, and the path on the west side of the point (left).

Short walks/picnic suggestions

1   **Tour de la Parata** (2.5km/1.5mi; 35min; ● easy; see violet lines on the map). Stroll around the tower, or climb up to it. This setting is best enjoyed under a setting sun, when the Iles Sanguinaires give off a pinkish glow, and all the day trippers have gone home.

2   **Pointe de la Corba** (2.8km/1.7mi; 1h05min; ● easy). Follow the main walk to the rocky cove just beyond the Pointe de la Corba (45min) and on the return head directly back to the car park/bus stop.

This walk is an excellent 'starter' and puts you into the holiday mood straight away. It's easy, gives you a taste of the beaches to come, and takes you through picturesque countryside. In spring you'll be intoxicated by the sweet-smelling maquis, when the hillsides are ablaze with a riot of brightly-coloured flowers.

The walk begins at the VISITORS' CENTRE at the **Pointe de la Parata** (●). This rocky promontory is the site of a 17th-century Genoese tower, built as a defence against the Moors. Beyond the point lie the Iles Sanguinaires, a group of sharp granite islets.

55

(There are several suggestions for their name, including their reddish hue at sunset: *sang* being the French word for blood.) Join the crowds — this walk has become massively popular in the last few years — and take the narrow lane on the east side of the peninsula out to the restaurant/souvenir shop (❶; **15min**). Decide now if you are going to detour to the tower: if so, add about half an hour to the walk timings.

Now take the GRAVELLY PATH at the left-hand side of the restaurant; you're immediately swallowed up in maquis, a low mat of Mediterranean scrub. An array of spring flowers holds your attention all along, and yellow spiny broom lights up the hillsides. You head round into a aquamarine-coloured bay, set at the foot of dark green hills. Vivid carmine *Lampranthus* covers the banks.

Rising past a maze of paths coming from the Visitors' Centre, you will see your ongoing route ahead: a dirt track following the west coast (**25min**). It's locally called the 'Customs Officers' Trail' — the **Sentier des Douaniers**. Make your way over to it and follow it along the coast, maybe in the company of the odd car bumping along to one of the flower-filled weekend retreats. Notice the pink-and-yellow-coloured rock on the hillock over to the left. After crossing a low crest above the **Pointe de la Corba** (❷; **45min**), you look down into a small rocky cove. The track descends to it (a good place to end Short walk 2 with a picnic), but you bear right, along the wide path. Lizards galore dart across your path, as you brush your way through flowers.

As you cross over a ridge (**1h15min**), a superb view greets you: two beautiful beaches rest in the now-flat coastline: the first is small and circular, the second large and sweeping. The white sand glares in the sunlight. An open grassy valley, sheltered by high rocky hills, empties out into the bay. The arm of the cape rolls gently out to the left. Descending, you soon come to a track above the first cove, to find the little holiday hamlet of **Capigliolo**. Make your way down the steps by the wall and onto the beach, the **Plage de St-Antoine** (❸; **1h27min**).

At the end of this blinding-white cove, squeeze through the rocks and mount the bank to continue along the shore. Just beyond the next cove, a path leads you to the **Anse de Minaccia** (❹; **1h40min**). The countryside here is completely unspoiled. Cows graze in the fields, and naturists loaf on the beach. I'll bet I know which gets your attention first!

It's possible to continue along the coast for another hour or more, to take in more inviting, usually-deserted coves. But the main walk ends here: return the same way to the **Pointe de la Parata** (**3h05min**), or take the inland route via the track from Capigliolo (Alternative walk 1).

Walk 2: ROCHER DES GOZZI

Distance/time: 5.5km/3.4mi; 2h30min

Grade: ●❗ moderate, with an ascent/descent of about 300m/1300ft. The paths are slippery when wet. You must be sure-footed and have a head for heights to reach the rock itself. Add another 100m/300ft of ascent if you detour to Punta Pastinaca before returning (**b**; *not recommended in mist*). *No waymarking*

Equipment: as page 50; walking boots, sun protection, long trousers and ample water recommended; *IGN map 4153 OT*

Access: 🚗 to/from the San Chirgu chapel in Appietto (42° 0.610'N, 8° 46.089'E). From the Col de Listincone on the D81, take the D581 north towards Appietto, and turn off right on a lane/track to the chapel just before the village cemetery. Or 🚌 (Timetables 2, 3) to/from the Col de Listincone (**a**), then on foot: 2.5km/1.5mi; 200m/650ft of ascent/descent; adds 50min overall.

The Rocher des Gozzi is the most noticeable landmark in the Gravona Valley northeast of Ajaccio. Every time you leave the town, there it stands — a solid mass of bare rock rising straight up off the plains. The best time to end this walk is in the evening, when the soft rose colour of the rock intensifies under the fading light. The stupendous panorama from the summit is ample reward for the climb the walk entails.

Start out at the **Chapelle San Chirgu** (**o**) in **Appietto**. From here you have a fine view of Appietto, a village dating from the Middle Ages, once the home of the Counts of Cinarca. It consists of three separate hamlets: the highest, with its miniature castle, and the lowest, with its lovely mansions, are the more picturesque.

From the parking area walk towards the radio mast, but turn right through a large wooden GATE just before it, then immediately head uphill to the left. In spring this path may be quite overgrown until it becomes established. As you ascend to the spine of the ridge, the hills fold back, and the vast Golfe d'Ajaccio comes into view. On your right you look down onto the Lava Valley, ensconced in the hills running up from the Lava Gulf. The Punta Pozzo di Borgo is the highest of these hills, and the isolated Château de la Punta stands out, perched on its slopes. It belongs to the Pozzo di Borgo family, descendants of Charles André Pozzo di Borgo, Napoleon's great enemy.

Heading east along the ridge and brushing through the dense flora, watch for tiny pink butterfly orchids. After passing through a GATE (**1**) you're on the right-hand flanks of the ridge,

Rocher des Gozzi from just below the Col de Listincone

and a ROCK 'BALCONY' serves as as excellent viewing point minutes later (❷; **35min**). Fifteen minutes later you may notice a path coming in from Punta Curbajola joining from the left (❸; **50min**).* Rounding a fold in the slope, you look straight across to the impressive rock … and Ajaccio. The way divides once in a while, so just contour, following either path. The hillside drops off into a precipitous wall down to the plain.

In half an hour you're on a saddle alongside the STONE RUIN (❹; **1h20min**) glimpsed from your earlier viewpoint. The **Rocher des Gozzi** sits directly behind it. A few minutes across, scramble down into a gap slicing across the neck of the rock. Ravines now fall away on either side of you. Notice also the pinnacle of rock bursting up on your right. All fours are needed, if you really want to explore. *The way is vertiginous — and potentially dangerous when wet — from here on.* Scant remains of stone walls appear — part of a medieval CHATEAU (❺; **1h35min**) that once belonged to the Counts of Cinarca. And what a view you have: you 'hang' straight out over the Gravona Plain and look towards Ajaccio's gulf and up to Monte Renoso. Watch the swifts swooping in and out and the lizards hunting, before you return the same way to the **Chapelle San Chirgu** in **Appietto** (**2h30min**) — or a little over **3h** if you made a detour up to Punta Pastinaca (❻).

*This path originates on Punta Pastinaca and *could* be used for the return if you take the detour to that viewpoint (fine outlook to Monte Cinto and Monte Rotondo), but it was badly overgrown when last checked and, despite some faded red waymarks, is definitely *not* recommended in mist.

Walk 3: FORET DOMANIALE DE CHIAVARI

See also photograph page 15

Distance/time: 9km/5.6mi; 2h20min (11km/6.8mi; 3h with detour)

Grade: ● easy walk on forestry tracks and trails; overall ascent of 150m/500ft (or 200m/650ft if you include the detour from the old prison). But on bright days the forestry tracks can be blindingly white

Equipment: walking shoes/trainers, bathing things; *IGN map 4153 OT*

Access: 🚗 or 🚌 (Timetable 6) to/from Verghia. Motorists can park at the signposted forestry footpath on the D55, 1km east of Verghia (on the north side of the Ruisseau de Zirione; 41° 48.664'N, 8° 46.512'E). Travelling by bus, alight at Verghia and walk back along the D55 for 10min to the Zirione bridge.

Short walk/picnic suggestion: Sentier du Myrte (2.5km/1.5mi; 45min; ● easy). This signposted forestry circuit through maquis and a cork oak wood (photograph page 15) is waymarked with wooden posts bearing a myrtle leaf motif (one of the constituents of the maquis). Keep left at a fork 10min uphill. After crossing a stream, the path passes an old mill: this is a lovely picnic spot, but there are also benches under the trees.

This walk takes you through a magnificent forest of cork trees, kermes and holm oaks, eucalyptus and maquis, to Chiavari's old prison. Birdsong accompanies you throughout the walk, which ends on the lovely nature trail in the intimate cork oak wood shown on page 15.

The walk starts at the PARKING AREA (○) for the nature trail (Sentier du Myrte) on the north side of the bridge over the **Ruisseau de Zirione**. Walk south over the bridge and after 100m/yds, turn left uphill on a forestry track. Ignore any forks to the right, and you'll come to a T-JUNCTION in a clearing (❶; **15min**). Turn right uphill here (the level track to the left is followed later, when you return from the prison).

You pass a small fenced-in GRAVEYARD on the right (❷; **35min**); continue straight ahead at the junction a couple of

A lovely 'avenue' of eucalyptus trees (top left) leads you to the grim old Chiavari Prison (bottom left). The prison's water supply building (top right) is still visible, and the building where gunpowder was made is some 300m north, on the D55.

minutes later. The track widens into a grand 'avenue' bordered with eucalyptus trees, and you soon come to the D55. Across the road is the **Ancien Penitencier de Chiavari** (❸; **1h**).

The history of the prison is as grim as the building itself. Of the 200 original prisoners in 1855, 82 per cent died in the first year, due chiefly to the poor hygienic conditions. Later the prison had up to 800 inmates, who worked the land nearby. Many were able to escape, usually with the help of the local people. The prison was closed in 1906. If you have time, you can take a 40-minute detour here (see purple line on the map), just to enjoy the woodlands and birdsong (up to 60 species of birds have been identified in this area).

When you've had your fill of history and nature, return to the track by which you arrived (be sure not to take the higher, motorable track which runs parallel with it for some 200m). Return through the arching eucalyptus and past the GRAVEYARD, back down to the junction first encountered at the 15min-point (❶; **1h30min**). Turn right here on the level track, and contour through the shady valleys. A little over 2km/half an hour along, ignore a CLEAR PATH (❹) down to the left. Just past here, by a couple of Forestry Department marker posts, you can see across the Zirione Valley and have a view down left to the Anse Ottioni, the bay where you set out. About four minutes later (somewhat over 200m/yds further on), you come to a junction where two paths go left downhill (the track continues inland, but ends in about eight minutes). Take either path down to the **Ruisseau de Zirione** (❺; **2h10min**).

After crossing the stream on stepping-stones, waymarks on the far side take you curling up left, and you join the **Sentier du Myrte** (❻) in a few minutes. Up to the right is an old RUINED MILL (ⓐ). Turn left on this nature trail* and, at a junction by a marker post with a myrtle leaf motif, keep right, to cross another little stream. Rise up to a CROSSING PATH (❼), where there is an electricity pylon over to the right; keep left here, back to the CAR PARK on the D55 (**2h20min**).

*Or, to see more of the nature trail, turn *right* here, pass the old mill, and follow the marker posts back to your car (the Short walk in reverse).

Walk 4: FORET DOMANIALE DE VIZZAVONA

Distance/time: 8.5km/5.3mi; 3h50min (add 1h if travelling by train)

Grade: ● moderate-strenuous, with some short steep scrambles. Ascent of 450m/1475ft. Can be very cold and *dangerous when wet*.

Equipment: as page 50; walking boots and bathing things recommended; *IGN map 4251 OT*

Access: 🚗 or 🚂 (Timetable 21) to/from Vizzavona. Travelling by car, park almost opposite A Muntagnera, an *auberge* 400m east of the Col de Vizzavona on the T20 (42° 6.872'N, 9° 7.264'E). From the railway station, take the road uphill to the right, signed (among others) to the Cascades des Anglais, GR20, Pin Laricio nature trail). *Carefully* follow the red/white GR waymarks and wooden posts with a pine tree motif to the bridge over the Agnone, cross it, and pick up the main walk at the 15min-point (add 30min).

Short walks/picnic suggestions

1 **Cascades des Anglais** (● easy; ascents of about 100m/330ft). Either follow the signposted trail to the Cascades des Anglais/Sentier Thématique du Pin Laricio from the railway station (**7**) and back (see above; 5km/3mi; 1h30min), or follow the main walk to the 30min-point (**4**) and back (3.4km/2mi; 1h). Picnic at the *cascades*, in shade or sun.

2 **Ruined fort** (4km/2.5mi; 1h05min *from A Muntagnera*; ● moderate, but you must be sure-footed; walking boots recommended). Follow the main walk to the 30min-point at **4**, then take the path on the left (cairn). This heads back southeast above the GR, contouring through a cairned rock chaos and then beech woods. In 15min, at a Y-fork, turn right, up to the top of the ridge and a ruined fort (**8**). Follow the good path (yellow waymarks) east along the ridge, but fork right after a few minutes, down to the T20. Turn left, back to A Muntagnera.

The cascading Agnone River is the essence of this walk. It bounds down a valley of rock into deep emerald-green pools. Monte d'Oro (2389m/7835ft), Corsica's fifth highest peak, dominates the valley. An apron of pines stretches around its lower slopes, but the valley itself is the home of a splendid beech forest. Of all these beautiful gifts of nature, it's the river you'll remember ... and the dazzling Cascades des Anglais.

Begin almost opposite the *auberge* A MUNTAGNERA. Walk

On the GR20, near Vizzavona station

down the track at the right of the PARKING AREA (**O**; YELLOW FLASH). Monte d'Oro soon appears through the beech trees. Its naked rocky crown rises high above the pine wood patching its inclines. When the track makes a U-bend down to the right, keep straight ahead on a path (**❶**) — to the crystal-clear bubbly river, with its green and alluring pools. The GR20 from Vizzavona crosses the BRIDGE here (**❷**; **15min**; seasonal KIOSK as well), while the nature trail keeps to the north side of the river.

Remaining south of the river, we now follow the GR. There is no single clearly-trodden path, so watch for the red and white waymarks. The Agnone bounces down the valley alongside you, one falls after another — the **Cascades des Anglais** (**❸**). At the top of the last cascade, a large CAIRN (**❹**; **30min**) on the left alerts you to a path back to A Muntagnera *(Short walk 2)*.

The route is very steep at times; sometimes you'll be using all fours. Green lichen illuminates the surrounding rock; under direct sunlight it glows with the fluorescence of a highlighter pen. Ignore a turn-off to the left at the **Bergeries de Porteto**, then cross the river on a FOOTBRIDGE (**❺**; **1h40min**), above a small but thundering waterfall. When you come to the scant remains of the old French Alpine Club (CAF) REFUGE (**❻**; **2h**), the spring snow-line is not far out of reach. Just below this small crumbled rock shelter is the largest waterfall in the valley. You're completely encircled by mountains — the Monte Renoso chain may still be wearing a mantle of snow.

The walk ends here at the refuge. (If you have time, you might like to continue on the GR20, or climb Monte d'Oro to a viewpoint over the tiny, hidden Lac d'Oro. These strenuous paths are only recommended for experienced hikers who have the relevant IGN map.)

Heading back, don't miss the beryl-green pools in the valley floor; some are magnificent. But if you decide to swim, make sure the pools are safe before you hurl yourself into them; the current can be very strong. Return to the kiosk at the BRIDGE in 1h30min (**❷**; **3h30min**), then retrace your steps to A MUNTAG-NERA (**3h50min**). Or cross the bridge and follow the GR/nature trail to **Vizzavona**, where the RAILWAY STATION (**❼**; **4h15min**) is just downhill to the left.

Walk 5: BERGERIES DE TOLLA

Distance/time: 9km/5.6mi; 2h55min

Grade: ● fairly easy, with an ascent/descent of 290m/950ft, but not advisable in bad weather.

Equipment: as page 50 (sturdy shoes will suffice), bathing things; *IGN map 4251 OT*

Access: 🚗 to/from Canaglia (via the D23, about 5km south of Vivario). There is no car park; park neatly, well tucked in. Or 🚌 to/from Tattone (Timetable 21; adds 1.7km/30min each way). From the station, head north along the minor road past the hospital on the left. Ignore all turn-offs until you come to your path to Canaglia (probably indicated by a handwritten sign: 'Canaglia, GR20'). After crossing a bridge, you join the D23 and follow it to the village.

Cascade du Meli

Short walk/picnic suggestion: Manganello River (3km/2mi; 55min). Follow the main walk to the 25min-point (**❶**); return the same way. Ample shade; boulders to sit on.

I first did this walk in autumn, and what a splendour awaited me. The beech trees left me in awe with their golds and yellows. The streams and rivers were magnificent cascades, filled by the autumn rains. Deep in the valley a wisp of smoke curling above the trees led me to the Bergerie de Tolla, a lonely pastoral outpost. Entering it was like walking into a children's story book.

The walk starts at **Canaglia** (**❍**), a small hamlet high on a hillside between the pine forest and chestnut trees, overlooking the confluence of the Manganello and Vecchio rivers. Three tracks face you here: take the track on the right, signposted 'REFUGE DE L'ONDA', to head up into the valley. High rocky summits peer above the thickly-wooded walls. You cross a GATED BRIDGE (**5-6min**); then, when the track forks some 50m/yds further on, follow the orange flash waymarking of the Mare a Mare Nord down to the right (there may be a signpost: 'VERS GR 20'). Pass a faint fork off to the right and come to the narrow, thundering **Manganello River** (**❶**; **25min**). (Swimmers: take the strong current into account.) The way narrows here, and alders grow along the riverside.

After about an hour of gentle uphill walking, you round a bend, to see the **Cascade du Meli** on the left (**❷**; **1h20min**; see photograph page 63), and a bridge takes you over its cascading waters. The higher you climb, the more striking the colours become, especially in the beech forest up ahead. Not long after passing the waterfall, leave this path and cross the Manganello on the **Passerelle de Tolla** (**❸**), following a signpost for the 'BERGERIE DE TOLLA'. (On your return from the *bergerie*, provided you're not all puffed out, I do recommend wandering up the GR20 path to the left signposted to the 'REFUGE DE L'ONDA', for about 35 minutes. In autumn it's a must! You'll

The Bergeries de Tolla. These small stone dwellings in a grassy clearing create a setting straight out of a book of fairy tales. Watch out for the mischievous donkeys here. They wander over to greet you, full of innocence, and just as you try to slip past, they reach for a nibble of your … you know what!

soon find yourself in a dense wood where moss coats the trees and drips off the rocks. It could be a Japanese garden.)

The **Grottaccia River** joins the Manganello just where you cross it. Once again you'll be reaching for your camera, to capture the Manganello as it surges out of a rocky gorge leaving swirling beryl-green pools in its wake. The best swimming hole is just a couple of minutes downstream from the bridge. Once over the river, your waymarking changes to the red and white flashes of the GR20. The livestock have created their own trails here, so be sure to follow the waymarks carefully. Don't forget to look behind you: high on the mountainside you'll spot a beech wood, a spectacular fire of colours in autumn.

Heading through a gap in the hills, you enter an enclosed valley and stumble upon the 'story book' **Bergeries de Tolla** (❹; **1h35min**). In season you can usually get a light meal here. For most of you this will be far enough. However, even more spectacular scenery lies further up the valley. You could, for instance, continue for another 50 minutes or so, to where a SERIES OF CASCADES (ⓐ) leap and bound down the valley from pool to pool

— an ideal swimming spot. To get there, take the path to the right of the last house at the *bergerie*.

Otherwise, from the Bergeries de Tolla return the same way to **Canaglia** (**2h55min**) or the railway station at Tattone (4h55min), but don't forget to add on ample extra time if you continue up the GR20 beyond the *bergerie* to the cascades or you take the detour from (❸) towards the Refuge de l'Onda.

Walk 6: PONTE DI NOCETA

Distance/time: 8km/5mi; 3h15min

Grade: ● moderate, with overall ascents/descents of about 350m/1150ft

Equipment: as page 50; walking boots, swimwear recommended; *IGN maps 4251 OT, 4351 OT*

Access: 🚗 (park at the railway station) or 🚌 (Timetable 21) to/from Venaco

Short walk/picnic suggestion: Ponte di Noceta. Access by 🚗: the bridge lies on the D43, southeast of Venaco. Plenty of shade, boulders to sit on.

An inviting pool awaits swimmers; a profusion of spring flowers greets botanists; superb scenery entices photographers. But for all that, I'm sorry to say that after the spectacular train ride to Venaco, the walk is a bit of an anti-climax!

Start at the RAILWAY STATION in **Venaco** (◉): follow the road uphill, then take the first left turn (sign: 'PLACE STE-CATHERINE'). Follow the charming alley then head left down concrete (❶) until you reach the D143, by a sign for the **Mare a Mare Nord**. Turn left down the road for just 75m/yds, then take the orange-waymarked cart track at the right of the CROSS (❷; **15min**). After crossing a stream you join a track (descending from the campsite above) on a sharp U-bend: keep straight on, eventually beside the noisy **Vecchio River**. Continue to the **Ponte di Noceta** (❸; **1h**), for a swim and a picnic.

Then follow the Mare a Mare back uphill and retrace your outgoing route back to **Venaco** STATION (**2h15min**).

Walk 7: FROM VENACO TO VIVARIO

Distance/time: 18km/11.2mi; 6h15min

Grade: ●: quite strenuous (overall ascents/descents of 800m/2625ft). Long ascent of 580m/1900ft to the Bocca Murellu. You must be sure-footed and have a head for heights. *Dangerous if wet;* don't attempt in changeable weather.

Equipment: as page 50; walking boots, warm clothing, bathing things recommended; IGN *maps 4251 OT, 4351 OT*

Access: 🚂 (Timetable 21) to Venaco; return on the same train from Vivario

Short walk/picnic suggestion: Vivario — Muracciole — Vivario (6.5km/ 4mi; 1h50min; ● quite easy, but slippery when wet. Follow the waymarking carefully! Overall descents/ascents 260m/850ft; walking boots recommended). 🚌 or 🚂 (Timetable 21) to Vivario. From the large fountain with the bronze statue on the T20 in Vivario walk north downhill towards 'CORTE'. A minute along (just before the bar-glacier), turn right down concrete steps (signpost: 'CHAPELLE D'ARCA, NOCETA'; orange flash of the Mare a Mare Nord). Just past the back of the school, turn left down a concrete lane. Pass a house on the left, ignore a path turning sharply left downhill, and keep right down a cart track. Cross the RAILWAY on a bridge (10min) and 2min later turn right on a narrow path in front of the gate to a house. You descend in pitch-black shade. Cross the RAILWAY again (20min; cairn), then cross a stream on slippery stepping stones (25min). After recrossing the stream a minute later, the path curls up hillside. Ascending in deep shade, *carefully* watch for the orange waymarks (and cairns) on this convoluted path, as you pass through ruins and beside stone walls. You pass to the left of the **Chapelle Santa Maria** (40min) and descend to a creepered bridge three minutes later. Beyond the bridge, climb up to **Muracciole**, keeping left at all forks. The best picnic spot is near Muracciole's CHURCH or, on a hot day, down by the bridge just below Muracciole. Return the same way.

Traipsing along and over ridges, you cross unkempt hills foraged by a handful of cows and goats; otherwise you're likely to have little company on these old trails linking six Venachese villages.

Begin at the RAILWAY STATION in **Venaco** (❶): follow WALK 6 to the **Ponte di Noceta** (❶; **1h**), shown opposite. Cross the bridge and follow the D43 west for 200m/yds, then turn left on a farm track (orange waymarks of the Mare a Mare Nord). Ignore the field track off right about 130m along, but take the path on the right just past it, now walking between two tracks giving access to cultivated fields. Cross a track and keep to the path beside the small shady stream (initially with another farm track to your right). A little over ten minutes further on, beyond a GATE, the route turns right uphill between stone walls (❷; just before TWIN TELEPHONE POLES), to climb up to the D43. Turn left on the road for under 100m/yds, then turn off left, on a track signposted 'NOCETA'. When you reach a fork within five minutes, bear right uphill; 50m/yds along, bear right again, on a rough — rather overgrown, but well waymarked — path.

Entering **Noceta** (**2h40min**), keep left (south) uphill on the D43. Many old mountain villages like Noceta have undergone

Opposite: the much-loved swimming hole below the Ponte di Noceta

a transformation and are once again inhabited. A couple of minutes uphill you come to a FOUNTAIN (**❸**) with a charming old CHURCH behind it. Head up the steep lane to the right of the fountain. Some 150m/yds uphill turn left on a path (signs: 'VIVARIO', 'MURACCIOLE'. You cross a disused track a couple of times. Your panorama now extends across to the Venaco side of the valley. In spring a great profusion of flowers entertains you with its colours — blue, indigo, yellow, pink, and white.

Crossing the **Bocca Murellu** (**❹**; 824m/2700ft; **3h45min**), you're soon following an old mule track. Vivario comes into sight, ahead to your left, stretching across a wooded hillside. Monte d'Oro (Walk 4) rises sharply in the background. Keep left at the next two junctions. Muracciole lies ahead, crowned by its miniature château.

Some 400m/yds beyond the enchanting, crumbled hamlet of **Arca** (❺), a WAYMARKED PATH joins from the right (**4h35min**). But keep ahead: cross a small BRIDGE draped in creepers and climb into **Muracciole** (❻; **5h**). The place has a timeless air; it exudes charm. The château rises behind the FOUNTAIN, which is shaded by a fragrant lime tree.

Top: Bocca Murellu. The longest climb in the hike rises to this pass — a steady pull of 580m from the Ponte di Noceta

Making for Vivario, return to BRIDGE and keep left at the Y-fork beyond it. In three minutes pass to the right of the solitary **Chapelle Santa Maria** (❼). Watch the orange waymarks carefully on the next stretch, as you pass crumbled buildings and walls. You slide down into a narrow valley in deep shade, crossing two streams. In spring, cyclamen shed some light in these pitch-black woods.

Fifty minutes from Muracciole you cross the railway. A wide path takes you up through a thin wood. Soon you join a track. A steep 10-minute climb sees you in **Vivario** (❽; **6h**). Head north towards Corte on the T20; the RAILWAY STATION (❾; **6h15min**) is 1km downhill: take left turn signposted 'GARE'.

Walk 8: SANTO-PIETRO-DI-VENACO CIRCUIT

See map opposite; see also photo page 4

Distance/time: 11km/6.8mi; 5h

Grade: ●❗ strenuous ascent and *very steep* descent of 850m/2790ft. You must be sure-footed, with a head for heights. *Less experienced walkers should descend from the Santo Eliseo chapel by the ascent route or do the walk in reverse. Do not attempt in changeable weather.*

Bergerie de Tatarellu

Equipment: as page 50; walking boots, sun-hat and warm clothing recommended; *IGN map 4251 OT*

Access: 🚌 to/from Santo Pietro (42° 14.753'N, 9° 10.363'E). Or 🚃 to/from Venaco (add 40min each way; Timetable 21).

Short walk/picnic suggestion: Sentier botanique de Caracatu (● 1h). Follow the walk across the bridge, then keep ahead up the lane to the signposted nature trail.

High on mountainside shelves you discover blissfully quiet pastoral outposts *(bergeries)* surrounded by lush grass. Cold mountain streams crash down the gullies around you, and your views expand with every step.

Start the walk at the CHURCH (❹) and FOUNTAIN in **Santo Pietro**. Follow the road at the right of the church uphill. At a T-junction, go right, crossing a BRIDGE (left is the return route). After 100m/yds, turn sharp right up a cart track (❶; orange flashes) and zigzag up through dense oaks. About 2km uphill, leave the track: take a steep path to the left (❷), passing the **Sentier botanique du Caracatu** and a SHEPHERDS' SHELTER: peek inside, to see how cosy this igloo-like structure is. Once out of the scrub, a magnificent view southeast over the confluence of the Vecchio and Tavignano valleys quenches your scenic thirst.

The ground is cushioned in moss as you near the alpine zone. Beyond a fork (keep right) you come to the **Chapelle Santo Eliseo** (❸; **2h30min**) and a *bergerie*. A sheer rock wall ahead seals off the interior of the island; streams gallop down on either side of the ridge.

Rising gently, you cross two streams, before gaining a small plateau and the **Bergerie de Codopratu** (❹; **3h20min**). The path crosses another stream and later contours round the hillside. After 1km, you are looking straight down into the Vecchio Valley, and the descent begins. *It's very steep and requires the utmost concentration.* The **Bergerie de Tatarellu** (❺), sheltering up against a beech tree grove on slopes illuminated by hellebores, is but a brief pause in this rocketing descent. Be sure to fork right for 'VENACO' not far past the last hut *and keep a careful eye on the waymarks.* I prefer this route, but you *could* take the violet-marked left fork for a more direct return. When you come to a T-JUNCTION (❻), go left, back down to **Santo Pietro** (**5h**). Or, if you've come by train, follow Walk 9 from ❻ (page 72).

Walk 9: THE VENACOS

See photo page 4
Distance/time: 8km/5mi; 2h35min
Grade: ● moderate, with ascents/descents of about 400m/1300ft overall
Equipment: as page 50; walking boots recommended; *IGN map 4251 OT*
Access: 🚌 to Poggio-Riventosa (Timetable 21; *request stop!*); return from Venaco. Or 🚂 to one of the stations and take the train to start the walk or return

Short walk/picnic suggestion: Circuit from Poggio (3km/2mi; 55min; ● easy). Access by 🚂 to/from Poggio-di-Venaco (D40 north of Venaco; 42° 15.404'N, 9° 11.112'E), or 🚌 to/from Poggio-Riventosa (Timetable 21; add 45min to overall time). Follow the main walk from Poggio (❶) to the viewpoint towards Corte in Riventosa (❸), then curl downhill to the D40. Turn left and, after 30m/yds, fork right on a footpath. This widens to a lane running above the road to the railway and takes you back to Poggio (❶). The Ruisseau de Taola, about 20 minutes from Poggio, is a lovely picnic spot.

This tour of the three Venacos is a gem. It makes a lovely complement to a journey on the little train. For the energetic, the whole 'Venachese' area, at the heart of the Parc Natural Régional, is a walking centre *par excellence*, a crossroads of the long-distance Mare a Mare Nord and several shorter locally-marked routes.

Start out at **Poggio-Riventosa** STATION (◉): follow the D140 uphill into **Poggio-di-Venaco** (❶; **25min**). Then, with your back to the cypress-framed WAR MEMORIAL, walk down the road ahead, at the right of an electricity transformer (walkers' sign: 'CORTE, CASANOVA'. In two minutes, as you pass below a CEMETERY on the left, go right down steps (CAIRNS, ARROW), to cut a bend off the road. Then, when the road makes a U-bend to the right, go left downhill on a path in deep shade (ARROW; CAIRN). Try to ignore the howling dogs up to the left as you cross a burbling stream on a FOOTBRIDGE (they are all penned in). After rising through a ferny dell, on the approach to Casanova, veer right to a tarred lane and follow it at the left of a stone hut with a house behind. Then the lane makes a U-bend to the left; there is a path ahead and another to the right. Before following the road uphill to the left, take either path to the **Ruisseau de Taola** (**45min**).

The road rises past a CAMPSITE and SPORTSGROUND on the left, as well as some new housing, to a FOUNTAIN and benches on the right, where you will see the first splashes of orange paint. You now skirt **Casanova**, where there are some traditional slate-roofed buildings on the left. Go straight over a crossroads onto a cobbled path (walkers' sign: 'RIVENTOSA, SAN PETRU') and, at a T-junction, turn left on another cobbled path. Rise up to the D140 and cross it (**50min**). Ignore a track to the left (by a TOMB with cypresses) and keep ahead towards Riventosa, spread out along a ridge above to the left. The path contours at the left of a drystone wall, then crosses another tinkling stream on a FOOTBRIDGE (**55min**) and passes the **Moulin de Riventosa** on the right (INFORMATION BOARD). Soon a shady track takes you up to **Riventosa**. Walk to the right of the CEMETERY, then curl up right on tar. Pass a lane off right signed to 'SAN PETRU' (❷; **1h05min**; you will return to this to continue the walk). Reaching the main D40 a minute later (TAP, WAR MEMORIAL), turn left up the cobbled road through the village kernel, passing to the right of the CHURCH. At a Y-fork, go right on a narrow road to a tremendous VIEWPOINT (❸) towards Corte.

Then return to the 1h05min-point in the walk (❷), the lane signposted to 'SAN PETRU'. *(But for the Short walk continue ahead.)* Follow the orange waymarks of the Mare a Mare to the T20 (**1h20min**). Turn right and walk to the junction with the narrow D340. Turn sharp left here, to pass the old CHÂTEAU POZZO DI BORGO on the left. Continue the gentle ascent on the D340, past a WAR MEMORIAL on the left, and keep right to come to the lovely CHURCH in **Santo-Pietro-di-Venaco** (❹). Now the easiest option is just to follow the Mare a Mare to Venaco, but it is mostly along the same narrow road. Why not try this higher route: walk up the road at the right of the church. At a T-junction by a BRIDGE (**1h40min**), go left, then turn right *twice* on tar to the top of the village. Walk up the signposted path to a Y-FORK (❺), where arrows point in both directions and take the path to the left (the return trail for Walk 8). This path, an orange-waymarked local walk, rises 100m/300ft and contours at about 900m, to a CROSSROADS OF PATHS (❻). Go left here, down to the T20 (**2h20min**), where you pick up the Mare a Mare again.

Follow the orange waymarks down into **Lugo**. If you don't want to visit Venaco, you can take a short-cut to the railway station: fork right on a stone-laid path behind the CHURCH (❼), down to the railway *line*. Walk right along the track for 150m, to **Venaco STATION** (❽; **2h35min**). If you *do* want to visit Venaco, from Lugo's church follow the D340 south to a Y-fork (just before Venaco's church) and go right, uphill, to the CENTRE (❾; the road left leads down to the station).

Walk 10: EVISA TO OTA (SPELUNCA GORGE)

See also photographs on pages 12 and 76

Distance/time: 7km/4.3mi; 2h25min

Grade: ● fairly easy, with a steep (although not difficult) descent of 620m/2030ft and ascent of 130m/425ft. Slippery in wet weather.

Equipment: as page 50; walking boots, bathing things recommended; *IGN map 4150 OT*

Access: 🚌 to Evisa (Timetable 3); return by 🚌 from Ota (Timetable 2)

Short walks/picnic suggestions: Ponte Vecchiu or Pont de Zaglia (up to 3km/2mi; 1h; ● easy; photographs overleaf). Access by 🚗: Park neatly at the side of the D124 below Ota, just north of the bridge crossing the Porto River (42° 15.372'N, 8° 45.896'E). You can see the Ponte Vecchiu as you descend from Ota; picnic there (20min return) or follow the orange waymarks east along the Spelunca Gorge and picnic by the Genoese Pont de Zaglia (35min each way). Shade, swimming holes.

The Spelunca Gorge is a must for every visitor. Imposing buttresses of pink- to violet-hued rock bursting up out of the valley dominate the landscape. Deep in the gorge, you wander alongside a tumbling river, crossed by old arched footbridges. In summer you'll be tempted to swim in one of the inviting pools. The walk ends at the delightful village of Ota, in majestic countryside.

You'll spend more time on buses getting to and from the walk than actually walking ... but the journey is through such superb landscapes that you can look forward to a splendid day out. **Start the walk** in **Evisa** (○), a high mountain village in a cloak of chestnut trees. Follow the road back downhill towards Porto for about 10 minutes, until you reach the END OF THE CEMETERY and a SIGN INDICATING THE VILLAGE EXIT. Already you will have noticed the rose-tinted granite peaks rising up out of the landscape.

A signpost, 'SPELUNCA', points to your path (❶). It is paved initially and waymarked with the orange flashes of the **Tra Mare e Monti Nord**. You dip down into a maquis wood sprinkled with pines, through which you can see the hillside village of Ota with its red-tiled roofs. Pink crags overshadow it. In the distance, the valley winds down to the sea. This old mule trail (slippery when wet) descends very steeply. Moss coats the surrounding trees, and the banks are flecked with cyclamen. Looking back, to the right, you see a bald mound of shiny grey rock bulging out of the summits. Soon precipitous, scrub-covered walls tower above you. Reaching the valley floor, you cross a stream on the beautifully-cobbled Genoese **Pont de Zaglia** (❷; **1h10min**), shaded by alders. The stream joins a fast-flowing river just below the bridge, and you may be tempted to swim. Soon the Capu di Larata (1193m/ 3915ft), Ota's guardian, holds your attention.

Crossing the D124 (**1h45min**), take the concrete lane off

left, down into the valley floor, rounding a FOOTBALL PITCH on the left and soon rejoining the river. A little over 10 minutes along, you cross the river on the **Ponte Vecchiu** (❸), a perfectly restored Genoese footbridge. The pool below it is ideal for swimming.

Over the bridge, swing left and follow the right bank of the river. Two mountains thrusting up from the valley ahead steal your attention. As you climb amidst swirls of grasshoppers, houses appear, stepped one behind the other on the hillside. Approaching Ota, keep to the path below the main road. This joins a lower road which takes you up to the main street in **Ota** (❹; **2h25min**) diagonally opposite Chez Féliz, a *gîte*. The bus leaves from the turning area by a FOUNTAIN just to the right.

But first look around, read the dates above the doors, and absorb the wonderful atmosphere of this charming, superbly sited village set below towering pink rock walls, amidst olive and fruit trees.

The Genoese Ponte Vecchiu (top) and Pont de Zaglia; both are ideal picnicking and swimming spots.

Walk 11: FROM OTA TO SERRIERA

See also photo on page 2   Distance/time: 12.5km/7.75mi; 5h

Grade: ●: strenuous, with an ascent of 560m/1835ft at the start, much of it very steep. The descent (875m/2870ft) is also very steep, and dangerous if wet. You must be sure-footed and have a head for heights.

Equipment: as page 50; walking boots, sun protection, bathing things recommended; *IGN map 4150 OT*

Access: 🚌 to Ota (Timetable 2). Return on the same bus from *Porto*. In high season (15/5-15/10) you can *flag down* a bus to Porto on the D81 at the Serriera turn-off (Timetable 8); otherwise you will have to walk (add 1h40min), or arrange a taxi. *NB:* If you're based at Ajaccio, this walk demands an overnight stay in Porto.

Alternative walk: If travelling by car, you may prefer to do an out-and-back walk to/from the **Bocca San Petru** (❼; 6h) — *well worth it!*

You set out overlooking the luxuriant, tree-smothered Porto Valley, and you end up in a landscape of dark rolling hills. In between, the route clambers up through a gap in the hills, where lofty, rose-coloured rock walls look down on you. All along the way you catch glimpses of the stunning Porto Gulf, of pink granite sea-bluffs, secluded coves and deep blue sea.

The walk begins in the centre of **Ota** (❹), where the bus turns round by a FOUNTAIN. Fill your bottles with water, then climb the cobbled road in front of Chez Félix (there may be a sign for the 'MARE E MONTI' trail). Turn left on the orange-waymarked trail at the first sharp right-hand bend in the road (❺), soon rising on steps and then swinging up behind the last houses. (A short stretch of path some 15 minutes along may prove difficult for inexperienced walkers.)

Superb views encompass you. Already high up, you look straight across the valley. Chestnut groves sprinkled across the slopes cheer up the dark countryside. Before you head around the hillside, take a moment to look back at Ota, with its bright orange-tiled rooftops and bib of grey-green olive trees. Soon Porto comes into view, trickling down to the sea alongside the final stretch of the Porto River. At the end of the village you can see a rock crowned with an ancient tower jutting into the sea (photograph pages 10-11). Minutes later, go right at the junction.

Mounting a RIDGE (**50min**), you look over into a narrow side-valley, where walls of rose-coloured rock seem to block your way. Looking back, you soon catch a glimpse of Porto's picture-postcard beach. Troupes of pink-flowering foxgloves flourish on rubble-strewn patches of hillside. Zigzagging back into this 'pink' valley, you scramble up through a narrow gap in rock

Above: Ota, with the cloven peak of the Capu d'Orto (Walk 15) and the higher Capu di u Vitullu in the background

walls, where the scent of the pale mauve-to-blue rosemary plants may surround you. When the path swings sharply uphill to the left, near the edge of the ridge (**2h20min**), there is a fine outlook over Porto's valley just to the right: the dome-shaped Capu d'Orto (Walk 15) dominates the landscape. Continuing up through pines and heather, you come into a spacious chestnut grove. A SPRING (**6**) is passed en route, and then a small stone building, up on the rocky hillock of **Pedua** to the left.

From here the path rises gently to a signposted pass (**7**; **Bocca San Petru**; **3h**). *(The Alternative walk retraces steps from here.)* A nearly-vertical descent follows … possibly on your backside. The countryside ahead eases out into smooth rolling hills but, inland, peaks still capped with snow appear in the distance. Further downhill, you spot the striking Bussaglia Beach, sprawling across the mouth of the wide, gravelly bed of the Vetricella River.

Clambering down a rocky ridge, you soon look straight down onto Serriera (**3h20min**). The village is as red as the hillside rock from which it was built. Pass through a lovely glade and then come out onto a TRACK (**8**). Remain on this track for 50 minutes, all the way to the MAIN PORTO ROAD (D81; **5h**). (Or follow the 'Mare e Monti' into **Serriera**, then walk along the D524 to the D81.) *Flag down* the bus at the JUNCTION OF THE D524 AND D81 (**9**; near the restored fountain shown on page 2).

Walk 12: CASCADES D'AITONE

Distance/time: 2km/1.2mi; 1h

Grade: ● easy, but you must be agile. Descent/ascent of 50m/165ft.

Equipment: as page 50; strong shoes, bathing things; *IGN map 4150 OT*

Access: 🚌 to/from roadside parking by fire-point sign 'EVI 05', on the north side of the D84 between Evisa and the Col de Vergio (42° 15.776'N, 8° 49.477'E)

Picnic suggestions: shade and tables on both the main and alternative walks

Extension: Chemin des Châtaigniers (●; 6km/3.7mi; 2h 15min). Our walk is part of a longer walk that starts in Evisa (❸) and follows the Mare a Mare, with information panels. Although not needed, a GPS track is available for download.

Alternative walk/picnic suggestions: Sentier de la Sittelle (3.2km/2mi; 1h10min; ●easy, very little ascent). This nature trail through Corsican pines and firs is 3.5km north of the 'Cascades' trail, at a fire-point sign, 'P79' (❹; 42° 16.315'N, 8° 50.732'E). It is waymarked with yellow flashes and wooden posts bearing a bird motif (the *sittelle: Sitta Whiteheadi*, the Corsican nuthatch). There are picnic tables at the parking area and by the Aitone. GPS track available for download.

Long a favourite spot for trout fishermen and swimmers, until 1905 the Cascades d'Aitone also powered three mills for grinding chestnut flour — once a staple of the local diet. This leg-stretcher is a delight of waterfalls glistening through a mixed wood of pine, fir, yew and beech.

Start out at the 'EVI 05' SIGNPOST (❍), where the Mare a Mare briefly joins the D84. Follow the roadside path north for 100m/yds, then bear left on the track behind the barrier (ORANGE WAYMARKS) and follow it to a picnic area with tables. Steps then take you down to the **Piscine d'Aitone** (❶; **15min**), a good picnicking and swimming spot.

Stay on the left (south) side of the **Ruisseau d'Aitone** and follow the rough path (agility required) beside the cascading river as far as the sign 'FIN DE SENTIER BALISÉE'. From here you have a fine view of the largest waterfall, the **Cascade de la Valla Scarpa** (❷; **30min**). One of the mills stood here; now there are only some walls and two millstones. Return the same way, passing two more RUINED MILLS, to the 'EVI 05' SIGN on the D84 (**1h**)... from where the 'CHESTNUT TRAIL' continues southwest to Evisa (❸).

Walk 13: LE CHATEAU-FORT

See also photographs on pages 12 and the cover
Distance/time: 1.5km/1mi; 1h
Grade: ● quite easy, but with many ups and downs, clambering over rock
Equipment: as page 50; *IGN map 4150 OT*
Access: 🚌 to/from the Tête du Chien (D81, under 4km north of Piana; 42° 15.178'N, 8° 39.441'E)

This short walk (with many picnic places) is characterised by whimsical eroded rock formations *(tafoni)* and superb vistas over Les Calanche and the Porto Gulf — from the tower all the way to the Gulf of Girolata.

The walk begins at the **Tête du Chien** (**O**; PARKING AREA, SIGN-POST; photograph page 12); it's waymarked (in yellow when last seen) and well trodden. It descends at first, then undulates along a ridge and rises to a ROCKY PLATFORM (**❶**; **30min**) looking out to Piana, the gulfs and marinas of Porto and Girolata and up towards Capu Tafonatu in the northeast above Walk 25. Close by is the 'Château-Fort', a castle-like rock pillar rising sheer from the valley below.

Return the same way to the PARKING AREA (**1h**).

Walk 14: LES CALANCHE

See map opposite; see also cover photo

Distance/time: up to 3.5km/2.2mi; 1h35min (just 1h05min by bus)

Grade: ● quite easy ups and downs (100m/300ft overall); some clambering requires agility

Equipment: as page 50; sunhat recommended; *IGN map 4150 OT*

Access: as Walk 15, page 80

Alternative walk: Three extensions to/from the *very busy* D81 are suggested (purple lines on the map), one a link to Walk 13. GPS tracks available for all.

Picnic suggestion: Lovely spots all along, but the only good shade is at the 50min-point.

Photo: Chemin des Muletiers (the old mule trail between Piana and Ota)

This short ramble is a brilliant introduction to Les Calanche and an ideal leg-stretcher for motorists. We follow part of the old mule trail between Piana and Ota. While much of it has succumbed to the D81, a good stretch of the beautiful stone-laid route still survives.

The walk begins at the *(request)* BUS STOP (❷) on the D81, 1km east of Piana. There's a sign here, STADE MUNICIPAL, and some WALKER' SIGNPOSTS. Follow the tar, then track to the CAR PARK and the stadium *(stade)* behind it. Then take the footpath running half-left across the stadium towards more signposts on the far side. Cross two FOOTBRIDGES and go left at the signposted fork just beyond the SECOND BRIDGE (❸). (A right turn here is a popular link to Walk 15's ascent of Capu d'Orto.)

On coming to a Y-fork in a small CLEARING (❹; **30min**), keep left to more signposts, then go straight ahead, following 'ANCIEN CHEMIN DE PIANA A OTA'. Now you pick up the old **Chemin des Muletiers** shown above, and it's nothing less than spectacular. Soon after rounding the ridge, you're greeted by mouth-watering views. The wine-coloured arm of Punta Scandola reaches out in the distance, while Piana slumbers in haze. Bits and pieces of the D81 thread their way through the rock pinnacles below.

You'll spot various old waymarks (some green, some blue dots on a white ground), but the path is easily seen. Sometimes you'll need to clamber. If you're planning to picnic, keep your fingers crossed that no one's already taken *the* spot — a large TREE WITH TWO FLAT ROCKS either side (❺; **50min**) — the *only shade* in this wilderness of rock.

Turn back now, before the path descends steeply, and retrace your steps to the CAR PARK (**1h35min**). But if you're catching a bus, continue the steep zigzag descent (slippery when wet) to the D81 beside a SHRINE to Santa Maria, then turn right and *flag down* a bus at **Les Roches Bleues** (❻; **1h05min**; bar/kiosk).

See also photographs on pages 10-11, 12 and 79

Distance/time: 12km/7.4mi; 5h45min (6h05min by bus)

Grade: ●❕ strenuous ascent/descent of 825m/2700ft. The ascent to the Orto summit at 1294m/4244ft involves some clambering and is only recommended for very experienced, sure-footed hikers with a head for heights. It can be very cold or cloudy, very dangerous in wet conditions.

Equipment: as page 50; walking boots, sun protection, warm clothing recommended; *IGN map 4150 OT*

Access: 🚗 to the 'Stade Municipal' car park off the D81, 1.6km south of Les Roches Bleues, 1km east of Piana (42° 14.404'N, 8° 39.265'E). If travelling by 🚌 (Timetable 2), this is a *request stop*; to return, catch a bus *from Les Roches Bleues.*

Alternative walks (GPS tracks available for all alternatives)

1 Foce d'Orto (10km/6.2mi; 4h10min; ● fairly strenuous; overall ascents/descents 700m/2300ft). Follow the main walk to ❸ (the 'Fontaine' junction, the 1h15min-point). Keep right and, at the faint fork 15min later, turn left. Eight minutes uphill you're at the **Foce d'Orto** (🅐) — a gap in the rock — with wonderful views of the inland hills and Evisa, high on a plateau. Return to ❸ to continue, but *ignore* the turn-off at ❹ for the Capu d'Orto.

2 Capu d'Orto from the Foce: Take the steep cairned path (●❕) from the **Foce** (🅐) to the **Capu d'Orto** (🅖; 1h); pick up the main walk at the 2h45min-point.

3 Alternative ascent: Take the popular violet-highlighted trail (●) on our map (blue waymarked). Turn right at the **Bocca Larga** T-junction (🅐) and about 5min later turn right at ❼ and pick up the main walk at ❹ (the 1h40min-point).

This walk turns the weird and wonderful weather-sculpted rock of Les Calanche inside-out for you. Heading inland from the Calanche, the landscape changes again, and you wind your way around massive mounds of bare pink and grey rock. From the summit of Capu d'Orto you the enjoy five-star views shown opposite.

The walk begins at the CAR PARK (◉) for the STADE MUNI-CIPAL. Walk back towards the D81 but, 50m short of it, turn left (east) on a track for 'CAPU DI U VITULLU' (❶). (Bus users startng at (🅐) turn right just 50m uphill at the Y-fork.) You pass a SIGN showing colour coding of the area's walks and soon enter a V-shaped valley lined with rocky hills, passing a WATER CATCHMENT on the left. The inclines on your left are pink; those to the right are grey. Capu di u Vitullu (1330m/4362ft) is the impressive mountain of rock dominating the right-hand side of the valley. Capu d'Orto is still hidden from sight by the ever-billowing mounds of rock on your left. Keep left at the Y-FORK (❷; **15min**). When the track ends (**35min**), take the wide cobbled path to the right (SIGNPOST). Heather and strawberry trees flank the way, and the path narrows as you ascend into pines. Within the next 15 minutes, ignore a faint turn-off to the left.

Some 25 minutes later you reach a junction where the word 'FONTAINE' (❸; **1h15min**) is carved in a rock. Branch off left here for 'CAPU D'ORTO' (orange waymarks). *(But go right uphill — also orange-waymarked — for Alternative walks 1 or 2.)* Soon wild rosemary, with its pale blue blooms and strongly-scented leaves, captures your attention. You head across a wooded basin, crossing a stream (usually dry).

Approaching the **Bocca di Piazza** (❹; **1h40min**) you come to your turn-off right for Capu d'Orto (green waymarks). Now you have to scramble up the rose-coloured rock, brushing through clumps of rosemary and watching out for the waymarks and cairns. Bizzarely eroded rock formations *(tafoni)* grow up around you, their colours intensifying. After less than 10 minutes' scrambling, the impressive peak confronts you, bulging straight up out of the landscape. A fine veil of bright

View from the summit of Capu d'Orto. For me, this is the most breathtaking viewpoint on the island. Porto sits far below, the whole gulf lit up by its beach. Beyond the Genose tower shown on page s 10-11, a rugged coastline twirls its way north, leaving behind small coves.

81

green lichen covers the rock face, which is separated from you by a shallow neck of pine-collared rock. You can take either of the two paths dropping down towards the pines.

You come to a slight groove in the hillside, where the words 'CAPU D'ORTO' and an ARROW pointing straight up (**2h15min**) appear in faded paint on the rock. From here on the way is marked by a 'museum' of CAIRNS. If you don't enjoy scrambling up a steep rock face (especially with the prospect of getting back down), call it a day here and just lap up the view. The heights of the Calanche bump their way seaward, getting more unruly and expressive as they go. Beyond this realm of pink rock, you see Piana wrapped in greenery, nestling high on a crest.

Those climbing to the summit will find hand-holds a help in tackling this 'groove'. Just when you think you're almost there, the twin-breasted peak looms up ahead ... still 25 minutes away! You cross a small GRASSY SHELF (**❺**; 1174) where the path from the Foce d'Orto joins, and then the final assault begins, again with the help of your hands. *Make sure all the rocks you stand on or lean against are secure!* Once in the cleavage of the split peak, clamber *carefully* up onto the right-hand protrusion — the SUMMIT of **Capu d'Orto** (**❻**; **2h45min**). The view is the most breathtaking that I have seen on all my walks on Corsica. Not only do you overlook Porto's sweep of beach and tower but, inland, great rounded hills roll back one onto the other. Evisa is seen, set on a plateau back in the hills. To the southwest, the vista stretches as far as the bays of Cargèse — the gulfs of Chiuni and Péru. A little further along to the right, you peer down onto Ota, resting at the foot of an amphitheatre of rose-coloured rock.

Descend back to the **Bocca di Piazza** (**❹**; **3h45min**) and head right on the far side, following the green waymarks. At a waymarked junction about five minutes later, keep right. You get another glimpse of Piana, this time framed between rocky outcrops and flowering scrub. Passing through a neat STONE WALL (**4h45min**), the bay reappears through trees. Just below lies a DELL OF CHESTNUTS and pines (**La Châtaignerie**), where you ignore a turn-off to the right. A few minutes beyond the dell, keep left (**❸**; green waymarks). Soon you're looking down into the valley you ascended earlier.

Descending through a clearing thick with cistus and heather, you reach SIGNPOSTS (**❾**; **5h20min**). *Motorists* head *left* here (green/blue waymarks), making sure to follow the path where it cuts back left a couple of minutes downhill. Beyond two FOOT-BRIDGES and a STADIUM, you're back at the CAR PARK (**5h45min**). *To catch a bus,* fork right ('ANCIEN CHEMIN DE PIANA A OTA') and follow Walk 14 from the 30min-point (page 79). *Flag down* a bus at **Les Roches Bleues** (**ⓑ**; **6h05min**).

Walk 16: CALVI • NOTRE DAME DE LA SERRA • LA REVELLATA • CALVI

See map overleaf and photos on page 85

Distance/time: 8.5km/5.3mi; 2h10min

Grade: ● fairly easy ascent/descent of 200m/650ft on good tracks and paths

Equipment: as page 50; stout shoes, sun protection, bathing wear recommended; *IGN map 4149 OT*

Access: The walk begins and ends at Calvi's railway station (35° 14.739'N, 25° 38.182'E).

Longer walk: La Revellata (15km/9.3mi; 3h 40min; ● grade as main walk, but long). Follow the main walk to the Plage de l'Alga (❹; 1h 30min), then go *left* on the coastal path. Beyond the largest cove (Anse de l'Oscelluccia), the path eventually rises to the lighthouse road. Turn right to the lighthouse (❹)at the end of the point. From here you could continue 0.5km to the Marine Biology Research Centre (❺): it's private, but access on foot is allowed (visits must be arranged in advance (www.stareso.com; tel: +33 (0) 6 86 22 32 61). Return the same way to the Plage d'Alga and pick up the main walk again.

Research centre and lighthouse at La Revellata

This delightful ramble is best enjoyed late in the day, when you can combine it with an evening picnic at the chapel, watching the fishing boats, yachts and high-speed ferries making for the port below Calvi's citadel.

Start out by following WALK 17 (page 85) up to **Notre Dame de la Serra** (❸; **50min**). Leave the chapel by heading due west — either on the access road or on the walkers' track to the right; 10 minutes down you pass some fascinating rocks — like the 'skull' shown on page 85). When the road/track forks, keep right and come to the main D81b (Porto road; **1h10min**).

Turn left here and, almost immediately, turn right on the track to the lighthouse on **la Revellata**. Soon you can take any of the paths or tracks down to the little cove below to the right (there are usually signs here, with the welcome word 'BAR' pointing the way). When you arrive at the beach (**Plage de l'Alga**; ❹; **1h30min**), indulge in a swim and some refreshment (although the bar may not be open outside high season).

Take the clear wide footpath from here all the way along the coast back to Calvi. The path ends at a road junction, where you turn right uphill on a narrow lane (❺). You pass below some wooden holiday bungalows on the right in about five minutes, then come to the coastal CALVI/PORTO ROAD (D81b; ❻) by the entrance to Résidence Tramariccia. Turn left on the main road and follow it past the CITADEL, back to the RAILWAY STATION in **Calvi** (**2h10min**).

Walk 17: CAPU DI A VETA

Distance/time: 14km/8.7mi; 5h10min

Grade: ● strenuous, with an ascent of 700m/2300ft. Only suitable on fine days *(dangerous in wet weather or with poor visibility)*. You must be sure-footed, with a head for heights. Inexperienced walkers should *ascend* on the descent route (see map): from the roundabout just east of the Casino supermarket, follow the road signed 'Pietramaggiore'. Turn right past the Hotel Corsica (on your right; 18min) and about 5min later, at a junction with private land ahead, turn left. After 250m/yds, just past a small parking area, take the narrow path to the left (red arrow, cairn).

Equipment: as page 50; walking boots, sunhat, warm clothing and plenty of water recommended; *IGN map 4149 OT*

Access: 🚌 to/from Calvi; 🚗 travelling by car, you can begin and end the walk at Notre Dame de la Serra; see footnote page 86.

Short walk/picnic suggestion: Notre Dame de la Serra (5km/3mi; 1h35min; fairly easy ascent/descent of 200m/650ft). Follow the main walk to the chapel above Calvi. Notre Dame de la Serra is an ideal place for an evening picnic,

Views of Notre Dame de la Serra, including the Capu di a Veta (left). This skull-like rock (bottom right) is on the motor road to the chapel.

when the sun bathes Calvi's citadel in a golden glow (photograph page 26-27). Picnic on the balcony by the chapel or on the hillock at the west side of the chapel. Then return the same way.

From start to finish, you have sweeping views over the Calvi Gulf. Scaling great swellings of hillside rock, and pushing your way through perfumed maquis, you reach the summit of the Capu di a Veta (703m/2305ft). From here you have a magnificent view over the gulf and the amphitheatre of hills behind it.

The walk starts at the RAILWAY STATION in **Calvi** (●): walk up steps to the main street (Avenue de la République), cross it, and turn left. Now take the first turn to the right (a wide trunk road, in front of the pharmacy). Then take the first left (signpost 'STADE'). Turn right in front of the stadium, then go left along-side the stadium (❶; sign: 'EDF'). When the road comes to a Y-fork just over 300m/yds further on, keep left on the road indicated as a cul-de-sac (another sign: 'EDF'). Pass two turnings to the right (the second gated) and, 50m/yds further on watch out for a small sign 'NOTRE DAME DE LA SERRA' at the right of the entrance to VILLA DE IRIS on your left (❷; **15min**). This sign directs you along a short passage leading to a climb over smooth rock with some steps. You rise to a field, where you can see the chapel, Notre-Dame de la Serra, ahead. Take the clear, maquis-lined footpath just to the right of the field. Sporadic orange and red waymarks take you all the way to the chapel, **Notre Dame de la Serra** (❸; **50min**).

Leave the chapel the way you entered it, and head left along the main track, towards the Capu di a Veta. At the fork 100m/yds along, bear right. Adorned with a cross, the peak fills

85

in the picture ahead. At the next fork, eight minutes later, go left. Another fork follows within 15 minutes; bear right (the way to the left is an optional return). Either continue on the main track to where it ends , or take the two waymarked short-cut paths, cutting out the hairpins. The track fizzles out at a pass overlooking a severe, rocky valley. Continue on the path opposite the nearby POWER PYLON (❹; **1h50min**). Head straight up, ignoring a path off left.

You climb steeply through a narrow passage in the ridge; small cairns and red dots mark the way. Once through the gap, you descend briefly. Scrambling round the rocky hillside, you edge along a ledge, where the going is a bit vertiginous. *Watch for the waymarks and go carefully on the loose stones.* Coming out to a cleavage in the ridge, you have views on both sides: Calvi and the gulf to the left and the unspoilt turquoise Nichiareto Bay to your right. Eight minutes later your views expand to encompass the enclosing arm of the Calvi Gulf — the Punta Spano. Lumio (Walk 18) is on the hills across the bay.

Ascending, remain on the left side of Veta's inclines until you reach the SUMMIT, the **Capu di a Veta** (❺; **2h45min**). Here you can sit back and take in this aerial view over the gulfs and surrounding hills. Mount Cinto, the island's highest point, is the shark's fin-shaped peak that rises out of the backbone of mountains. The Figarella and Fiume Seccu river plains form a vast fan around the bay.

Descending, take an easier route. Heading in the direction of Mount Cinto, find the red waymarks of your continuation (southeast, roughly 140°). Facing Calvi, descend the right-hand flank of the peak. You drop quickly, through a mass of vegetation. The path appears to come out at the end of a road, but in fact turns sharply right, descending into the bed of the **Ruisseau de Vivariu** (❻; **4h**), where you cross the stream and bear left. Keep your eye open for a few twists and turns in the path for the next 10 minutes, until you reach a road. Turn right downhill, cross a small stream, and go right at a junction (❼).* Turn left at the junction by the Hotel Corsica (❽) on the outskirts of **Pietramaggiore**. The main N197 is straight ahead, and the RAILWAY STATION just under 2km to the left (**5h10min**).

*If you go straight ahead here, after 200m/yds a red-waymarked path on the left (*not signposted* at time of checking) rises 175m/575ft through maquis back to your outgoing track, from where you could return to Notre Dame de la Serra, if you began the walk there.

Walk 18: CATERI • OCCI • LUMIO

See also photograph page 31(top left)

Distance/time: 8km/5mi; 2h15min

Grade: ● easy ascent (160m/525ft) and descent (200m/650ft); good tracks and paths throughout; *sparse* orange waymarking after the 1h-point

Equipment: as page 50; take a sunhat!; *IGN maps 4149 OT, 4249 OT*

Access: 🚕 taxi or with friends to the Couvent de Marcasso, near Cateri (35° 14.739'N, 25° 38.182'E); taxi back from Lumio (or 🚌 from Ondari, 4.5km southeast of Lumio on the N197; Timetable 12)

Alternative walk: Occi circuit (6km/3.7mi; 1h50min; ●moderate ascent; steep descent of 255m/835ft; *sparse* orange waymarking). 🚌 to the north entrance to Lumio on the N197; park just inside the road, opposite the Hotel Chez Charles (35° 14.739'N, 25° 38.182'E). Take the lane behind Chez Charles (**G**; sign: 'Village d'Occi'). This becomes a track, then a stone-laid mule trail which rises to the ruined village of Occi (**④**; 40min). From Occi follow a path which ascends southeast, then descends to a crossing trail (1h05min). Turn left to the little chapel of Notre Dame de la Stella (**❸**), then retrace your steps to this junction and keep straight on (due west), to descend quite steeply to Lumio.

Picnic suggestion: Occi (3km/1.9mi; 1h10min; easy ascent/descent of 165m/540ft). Follow the *Alternative* walk to Occi; return the same way.

D iscover the enchanting villages of the Balagne on foot. For a change you don't have to climb hundreds of metres for an unforgettable view; wonderful rural vistas accompany you all along these hills. See also Walk 19.

Start the walk facing the front door of the **Couvent de Marcasso** (**O**): descend the mule trail at the right of the garage. Heading above fields and beside tired stone walls, you arrive at **Lavatoggio** (**15min**). Walk up to the D71 and turn right. After about 25m/yds, climb steps on the left (**❶**; *not waymarked* when last seen). At the top, turn right on ALLÉE ROGER DASSONVILLE

Occi and its restored church

Notre Dame de la Stella: this chapel, one of the very few places on the walk where you'll find shade, was refurbished at about the same time as Occi's church was rebuilt.

(AREA MAP; red flash on a weight limit sign). You look back across the valley to the square church tower at Aregno and to Sant' Antonino straddling a hill (photographs pages 31 and 29). Continue up the lane, then track, to a tiny chapel, **San Giovanni di Venti** (❷; **30min**).

Keep on the track straight past this chapel, heading towards Capu Bracajo, until you come to another chapel, **Notre Dame de la Stella** (❸; **1h**). Keep straight ahead on the track past this chapel, too. Then, after 50m/yds, you can either take the cart track uphill to the right or continue for another 120m/yds and take the orange-waymarked path up to the right. (Straight ahead is the path to Lumio, to end the Alternative walk.) Ignoring any paths to the right, rise with fine views to Calvi, la Revellata, the Bonifatu mountains, and Capu d'Occi up to the right.

Beyond a pass below Capu d'Occi, the trail descends to the dramatically perched ruins of **Occi** (❹; **1h35min**). The village was probably founded in the 15th century by people living on the coast in uncertain times, who moved inland to flee pirate raids. By the late 1800s there were only 60 inhabitants left, and when the last died in the early 1900s, Occi was abandoned. In 2002 the church was completely restored, and services are now held once a year, at Pentecost. Local people do not want the village to become commercialised, so it is only accessible on foot.

From the church, walk towards a stone wall and then left, ignoring a good path on the right (it goes down to Camping Panoramic on the D71). Round the village to the north, to its northwest corner. Then descend the old stone-laid mule trail (**❺**; some orange waymarks), soon zigzagging down through pink boulders (**❻**; the **Calanche**). At a fork, take the track to the right. Coming onto a lane, follow it behind the HOTEL CHEZ CHARLES (**❼**), then fork left uphill into **Lumio** (**❽**; **2h15min**).

Walk 19: FROM SANT' ANTONINO TO L'ILE-ROUSSE

See map pages 88-89; see also photographs on pages 29 and 31

Distance/time: 9km/5.6mi; 2h10min

Grade: ● easy descent of 450m/1475ft on good tracks and paths. The way-marks are faint and infrequent, but the route is straightforward.

Equipment: as page 50; walking boots and sunhat recommended; *IGN maps 4149 OT, 4249 OT*

Access: 🚕 taxi or with friends to Sant' Antonino (42° 35.355'N, 8° 54.390'E); return by 🚌 from l'Ile-Rousse (Timetable 12)

Alternative walk: la Balagne (21km/13mi; 6h; ● moderate, but long; over-all ascent: 550m/1800ft; descent 650m/2130ft; *little shade*). Access: 🚕 taxi to Chez Charles in Lumio; return as main walk. Follow *Alternative walk 18* to the chapel of Notre Dame de la Stella (waypoint ❸ of Walk 18). Then use the map or our GPS files (do not rely on waymarking), remembering that you will always be on a lane or a *good* path (the remains of an old mule trail). Leaving Lava-toggio, turn sharp north opposite the church, down into Croce, then take the first right (the trail to the Couvent de Marcasso is only 25m/80ft below the road). Turn left at the chapel just before Cateri: the trail continues from below the Hotel San Dume. Go through Aregno to the Pisan Romanesque Eglise de la Trinité (12C), then climb to Sant' Antonino and pick up the walk below.

Picnic suggestions: Sant' Antonino (easy, 10-15min on foot, *but no shade;* best suited to an *evening* picnic). Walk up to the hilltop in the middle of Sant' Antonino (view to Algajola Bay, the inland mountains, and over Sant' Antonino itself), or follow the main walk to the view over Corbara.

Together with Walk 18, this short downhill ramble gives you a good overview of the Balagne. But if the weather is cool and breezy, then I heartily recommend the *Alternative* walk above — it's a 'grand tour' in every sense!

Start the walk in **Sant' Antonino**, at the village CAR PARK (**O**). Take the dirt track (WALKERS' SIGNPOSTS) to the left of the CHURCH, heading for a CEMETERY on a rise. At a fork about 200m/yds along, go right (left *may* be signposted to the Couvent de Corbara). This sandy track is *not* signed, but it affords better views and avoids an unnecessary climb in full sun from Corbara. You rise over a PASS and pass a track up to the relay station on **Capu Corbinu** (❶; **15min**). This is a brilliant viewpoint down over Pigna and Corbara, with the Couvent de Corbara in the foreground, backed by the Cima Sant' Angelo — a lovely picnic spot.

At a T-junction (**25min**), keep left downhill. Two minutes later the path from the Couvent de Corbara comes in from the left (❷; there is usually a barrage of signposts at this point, but they are often broken). Keep right here (you may spot the occasional waymark). As you pass below the **Cima Sant' Angelo**, you have a good view down to l'Ile-Rousse and its lighthouse; in the middle distance, cypresses and a slender church tower announce Occiglioni, the next village en route.

You soon pass a beautiful old RUINED CONVENT on the right (❸; **40min**). Palmento is the village just below to the east. Be sure to take a break under the venerable oak here — the only shade for miles around! Then follow the track into an S-bend. You'll be surprised when you see that you have *passed* Occiglioni's church! Don't worry, your turn-off back to the village comes up 700m/yds past the ruin: take the old mule trail down to the right (❹; **50min**). Yellow flashes guide you down past the village CEMETERY and WASH-HOUSE (both on the left), into **Occiglioni** (❺; **55min**). Walk to the left of the CHURCH on a beautifully cobbled path and then follow the cobbles downhill under an arch. Go straight ahead between the houses and in two minutes you come to the D263, by a viewpoint with an IRON CROSS.

Go down the concrete steps just to the left of the viewpoint (WALKERS' SIGNS). Keep left at two Y-forks. From up here you enjoy good views of your final destination. You pass a lovely (but dry!) FOUNTAIN on the left (❻; **1h10min**). A few cobbles underfoot remind you that this was once a beautiful old mule trail. But no more: just 20m/yds below the fountain an eroded access track has been bulldozed —at least it *was* quite awkward and rutted when last checked (2016), but it's waymarked in yellow every few feet, so there is no escaping it. Fifteen minutes down from the fountain you pass a signposted trail off right to 'ILE ROUSSE' (ⓐ; just 100m below a track off right signed 'Giro Occiglioni–Palmeto'). We didn't have time to walk this trail (which had been newly cleared), but we think it *might* be a more pleasant route than the 'official' route we take — which basically keeps straight ahead due north (see map), rounds a housing development and emerges on the main N197 by WALKERS' SIGNPOSTS (❼; **1h45min**). Turn right to **l'Ile-Rousse** (❽); after enjoying a drink in the plane-shaded square (photograph page 31), walk on to the RAILWAY STATION by the port (❾; **2h10min**).

View over l'Ile-Rousse

Ancient junipers growing in the dunes play an important ecological role, forming a screen behind which maquis and trees can grow.

See also photo pages 8-9   **Distance/time:** 6km/3.7mi; 1h45min

Grade: ● easy after a *very steep, rough descent* (including a ladder); *no shade*

Equipment: as page 50; sunhat, waders, bathing things, plenty of water; *IGN map 4249 OT*

Access: 🚌 to/from Ostriconi: the road runs north off the N1197 some 2.5km west of the Ile-Rousse/St-Florent junction to a campsite; park in one of the lay-bys above the beach, 1km off the N1197 (42° 39.487'N, 9° 3.577'E)

Picnic suggestions: coastal path (no shade), footbridge (shade nearby)

The Plage de l'Ostriconi lies at the western end of the Désert des Agriates and the Sentier du Littoral (see Walk 33). It is one of the few areas of dunes in Corsica and a 'textbook' habitat for plants and birds. The setting is magnificent; the Ostriconi River meanders through rich farmlands and trees to its mouth at a vivid turquoise sea, collared by a necklace of white sand (see pages 8-9).

The walk begins at the PARKING BAYS above the beach (**○**). Scramble down the steep path, then (outside summer) wade across the mouth of the **Ostriconi River**. Cross the **Plage de l'Ostriconi**. On the far side, rise up on a track, then fork left on the coastal path. After crossing a streambed, the path runs above two small RUINS (**❶**; **i Magazini**) and then two old stone pillars (navigational aids). You can end the walk at the **Anse de Vana** (**❷**; **45min**) with a swim, or follow the ongoing path as far as you like.

On your return take the SANDY INLAND TRACK (**❸**; arrow carved in stone). You pass a signboard for the SENTIER DU LITTORAL (**1h 10min**). A few minutes later, at a Y-fork, turn down to the beach. Walk along the back of the beach until you come to a juniper- and reed-edged creek. Follow the cart track beside it (again be prepared to wade) to a little FOOTBRIDGE (**❹**) over the **Etang de Foce** — an idyllic spot, with eucalyptus and farmland on the far side. Then retrace your steps to the PARKING BAYS (**1h45min**).

Walk 21: FROM CALENZANA TO BONIFATU

Distance/time: 11km/6.8mi; 4h

Grade: ● moderate, with a overall ascent of some 400m/1300ft

Equipment: as page 50; walking boots, warm clothing, bathing things, ample water recommended; *IGN map 4149 OT*

Access: �```taxi or with friends to Calenzana (12.5km from Calvi), or``` (Timetable 10; in *high season only*); return with the same taxi from the *auberge* at Bonifatu (or phone 04 95 65 30 36 for a taxi when you arrive).

This hike follows the start of the 'Mare e Monti' ('Sea and Mountains') footpath. In spring the maquis is a tangled bouquet of colour. As you near Bonifatu, you climb alongside the Figarella River, and will no doubt want to relax beside its inviting and invigorating pools.

Start in **Calenzana**, an important centre in the Genoese era. With your back to the baroque campanile of the 17th/18th-century church of **St-Blaise** (○), go up the alley at the right of the TABAC/BAR/GLACIER (another narrow street and the chapel of **Ste-Croix** are to the right, and there are orange (Mare e Monti) and red (GR) waymarks on a wall. You pass a BOUCHERIE on the right and rise to a higher square with the MAIRIE and a WAR MEMORIAL. Waymarks lead past the POSTE on the left and up into the QUARTIER DE L'EVÊQUE: it's worth looking around this area, with its beautiful old wooden doors and bookbinder's *atelier*. Signs and waymarks guide you to the right along a narrow street, then left up to the little **Oratoire St-Antoine de Padue** (❶) on the left. The waymarked path proper begins here.

When the GR20 eventually forks off left (❷; **1h**), keep right, following orange waymarks. You look out over the flat-bottomed valley of the Fiume Seccu. Once over the pass (**Bocca u Corsu**; ❸; 581m/1906ft) you drop down into the vast, tapering Figarella Valley, just where it disappears into the central massif. Not long after the third stream crossing, you come to a TRACK (❹; **1h50min**) and keep straight ahead uphill for 'BONIFATU'. A little over 1km along, past a turn-off to the left, you look up into rocky mountains.

Eventually the valley closes up, and you cross the **Figarella** (❺; **3h05min**). Here you leave the track and follow the river, turning left up a wide signposted path. Scramble along the old watercourse, briefly floundering across rocks and boulders and passing some inviting POOLS, the largest of which is just 100m before your turn-off (**3h25min**). It draws you to a halt, and you soon forget the time. Cool off, then bake yourself dry on one of the gigantic boulders! No need to hurry; the walk ends only 35 minutes uphill.

A rough 15-minute ascent brings you onto the Bonifatu road at **Bocca Reza** (❻); turn left here. After 150m you pass a path off right (part of the circuit followed in Walk 23). You now look

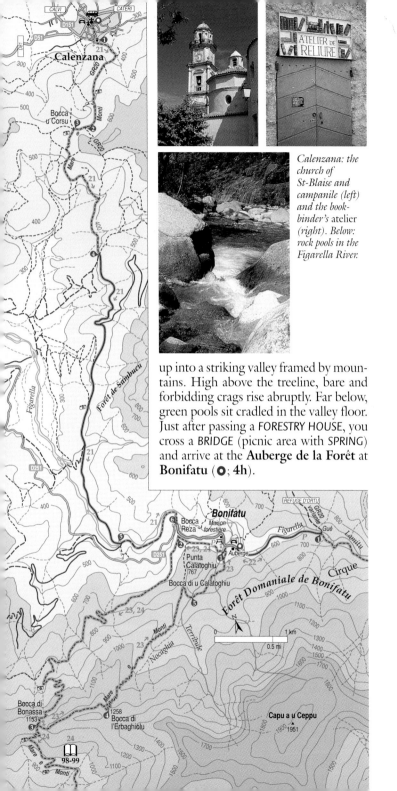

Calenzana: the church of St-Blaise and campanile (left) and the book-binder's atelier (right). Below: rock pools in the Figarella River.

up into a striking valley framed by mountains. High above the treeline, bare and forbidding crags rise abruptly. Far below, green pools sit cradled in the valley floor. Just after passing a FORESTRY HOUSE, you cross a BRIDGE (picnic area with SPRING) and arrive at the **Auberge de la Forêt** at **Bonifatu** (○; 4h).

Walk 22: BONIFATU • REFUGE DE CARROZZU • SPASIMATA BRIDGE • BONIFATU

Distance/time: 14km/8.7mi; 5h45min

Grade: ● fairly strenuous, with an ascent of 740m/2430ft lasting two hours. Not suitable in cold or changeable weather. While the descent to the Spasimata suspension bridge might prove unnerving for some (❀), *I heartily recommend this walk to anyone who is fit and sure-footed — even beginners.*

Equipment: as page 50; walking boots, warm clothing, bathing things and plenty of water recommended; *IGN map 4149 OT*

Access: 🚗 car from Calvi via the airport road and the D251, to/from the *auberge* at Bonifatu (22km; 42° 26.541'N, 8° 51.278'E); paid parking in season

Shorter walks/picnic suggestions: ● Follow the main walk to the 20min-point (**Ruisseau de Lamitu**) or the 50min-point (**Ruisseau de Meta di Filu**). Good streamside picnicking, in sun or shade. (There is also a shady picnic area, with a spring and stone table just by the bridge at Bonifatu.)

Y ou scale the wall of a deep valley in the shade of a forest, with the sound of tumbling water following you all the way. Rock pinnacles tower above you, streams cascade across your path, and two suspension bridges add a touch of excitement.

The walk begins at **Bonifatu.** Head up the wide forestry road, with the **Auberge de la Forêt** (**O**) on your right and the boulder-strewn **Figarella River** below on your left. A thick blanket of trees covers the slopes. The track peters out by a ford (**❶**; **25min**) on the left over the **Ruisseau de Lamitu**, signposted to the 'Refuge d'Ortu di u Piobbu 3h'. Here we go uphill to the right, on a signposted, yellow-waymarked path. Up ahead, the valley forks, and an imposing pyramid of rock splits the ravine. Snow may still linger on the peaks.

A stream is crossed (**Ruisseau de Meta di Filu**; **❷**; **50min**); then you cross the **Ruisseau de Spasimata** on a first SUSPENSION BRIDGE (**❸**; **1h15min**). Wire ropes act as 'hand-rails'. On the far side of the river, your ascent becomes more noticeable. Two more stream crossings follow.

You pass the remains of hillside terracing and a stone table and benches beside the stream (**2h**). A small STONE SHELTER lies a couple of minutes further on. Go steeply uphill, to another signposted junction. The refuge is left; Asco and the Spasimata bridge

right. First go left. You walk into a picture postcard. Over the hillside birches and pines, you have views of the lush plains far below, framed by the near-vertical valley walls. A sloping hill of smooth rock slides down on your right, and behind it, in complete contrast, a sharp wall of rock cuts across the landscape. A cone-shaped peak looming up across from you dominates the scene. The wonderfully-sited **Refuge de Carrozzu** (➍; **2h 30min**) sits just around the bend. For the use of overnight visitors only, it's fully equipped and open all year, but only manned from June to October (when the guardian will usually only sell refreshments to GR20 walkers).

Returning to the signposted junction, follow the *GR20* (red and white flashes) towards Asco. You descend towards the valley floor (gripping chains help you on the awkward passages). The **Spasimata suspension bridge** spans the river just below you now. A cascade splashes down into the beautiful pool 20m/60ft beneath it. This is a very exhilarating spot. A chain helps you down the final drop to the bridge. If crossing the bridge 'gives you the jitters', don't look down through the slats — look up into the distance. Once over the BRIDGE (➎; **2h55min**), you can always wander a bit further on, following the GR20 towards Asco, but the going gets very tough. Picnicking beside the pool here is very popular 'in season'. From every angle the mountain scenery is tremendous.

Return to **Bonifatu** by the same route (**5h45min**).

This bridge over the Spasimata was replaced by a sturdier model in the late 1990s; nevertheless, only two people should be on it at one time.

Walk 23: ERBAGHIOLU CIRCUIT

See map pages 94-95 | **Distance/time:** 11km/6.8mi; 5h

Grade: ●❗ strenuous, with an ascent of 760m/2500ft; you must be sure-footed and have a head for heights

Equipment: as page 50; walking boots, warm clothing and water recommended; *IGN map 4149 OT*

Access: 🚗 car from Calvi via the airport road and the D251, to/from the *auberge* at Bonifatu (22km; 42° 26.541'N, 8° 51.278'E); paid parking in season

H uffing and puffing up to the pine woods and grassy slopes, you look out along the winding Figarella Valley to the Gulf of Calvi, before disappearing back into the forest on your return to Bonifatu.

Begin at the **Auberge de la Forêt** (**O**) at **Bonifatu**. Walk back along the D251 then, just before the bridge, turn left on the signposted and orange-waymarked 'Mare e Monti' trail. Just over 100m up, turn right on a PATH (**❶**) which rises slightly below **Punta Calatoghiu**. Ignore the path to the left rounding that peak (a pleasant short circuit). Take the *next* path on the left (**❷**; RED WAYMARKS). From here you'll be climbing for two hours; small streams make good resting places en route. As you leave the woods, Calvi — just a smudge of white — and the gulf are glimpsed through the hills. Cyclamen, violets, and buttercups lie along the path; moss and grass cushion the hillside. The air is fresh, and the odd fir tree enhances this alpine atmosphere.

Knees-a-quiver, you pass a SPRING on the left not far below the **Bocca di Bonassa** (**❸**; 1153m/3780ft; **2h20min**), the highest point on the 'Mare e Monti'. A dip in the distant hills reveals the Fango Valley and scattered habitations (Walk 24). You meet the 'Mare e Monti' again at this pass: now follow its orange flashes and the red waymarks to the highest pass on this walk, the **Bocca di l'Erbaghiolu** (**❹**; 1195m/3920ft; **2h55min**).

Then begin the steep zigzag descent down to the upper reaches of the **Ruisseau de Nocaghia** and follow it down the valley, with the sound of rushing water below through the trees. After crossing this stream (**❺**; **4h25min**), continue down to the BRIDGE and turn right, back to the **Auberge de la Forêt** at **Bonifatu** (**5h**).

At the Bocca di Bonassa

Walk 24: FROM BONIFATU TO TUARELLI

Map begins on pages 94-95 and ends below

Distance/time: 19km/11.8mi; 6h15min

Grade: ●❘ strenuous climb of 620m/2035ft at the outset; the rest is a doddle … but long. You must be sure-footed and have a head for heights. Not recommended in changeable weather.

Equipment: as page 50; walking boots, sun protection, warm clothing, bathing things and *plenty of water* recommended (the *only* source of water en route is the spring below the Bocca di Bonassa); *IGN map 4149 OT*

Access: 🚗 taxi or friends to the *auberge* at Bonifatu (42° 26.541'N, 8° 51.278'E); return with the same driver from either the Pont de Tuarelli-Chiorna on the D351 south of the Fango River (42° 23.201'N, 8° 44.737'E) or from the nearby *gîte* (Auberge l'Alzelli; only open May-September; 42° 23.208'N, 8° 44.976'E).

Alternative walk: Bocca di Bonassa (12km/7.4mi; 4h05min; ●❘ strenuous, with an ascent of 620m/2035ft. You must be sure footed, with a head for heights. Not recommended in changeable weather. Equipment as for *Walk 23*. Follow *Walk 23* (map pages 94-95) to the Bocca di Bonassa; return the same way.

Short walk/picnic suggestion: Fango River (7km/4.3mi; 2h30min; ● easy). Stout shoes will suffice, but take a sun protection and swimming things. 🚗 Park on the Fango River road (D351), either at the first bridge (**⑦**; **Ponte Vecchiu,** 2.5km from the D81, 42° 23.791'N, 8° 42.850'E) or the second (**⑤**; **Pont de Tuarelli-Chiorna**; 5km from the D81; 42° 23.201'N, 8° 44.737'E). In either case, cross the bridge to the north bank of the Fango, and follow the orange-waymarked 'Mare e Monti' to the other bridge, then return the same way. From the beautiful arched Ponte Vecchiu the path is signposted '*TUARELLI*'; from the second bridge you must first walk left uphill on a lane, to a signpost for '*GALERIA*', then turn left. (A right turn leads to the Auberge l'Alzelli (**⑥**); a simply idyllic refreshment stop.) There are picnic spots galore on this route, many with ample shade. About halfway along in either direction, you come to an exquisite river setting, where pale green-to-blue pools are set deep in a riverbed of rose-coloured, grey, and mauve rock. There are also irresistible swimming spots at each bridge.

This walk begins its descent where Walk 23 first pauses for breath — at the Bocca di Bonassa. You lose sight of the Figarella Valley, but the landscape opens out to another valley, equally as long, where the magnificent Fango River flows. If you've always preferred the sea to a river for swimming, you might just change your mind! The suggested Short walk makes a perfect 'river day', as opposed to a 'beach day', and is ideal for picnicking.

Begin by following Walk 23 (page 97) to the **Bocca di Bonassa** (**③**; **2h15min**) — the highest point on the 'Mare e Monti' trail, which you join at this pass. Now follow *orange* waymarks into a very steep zigzagging descent (perhaps on your backside in wet weather). *Watch the waymarking all the way!* A rocky nodule some 200m/650ft downhill, on a deep bend, affords a good view down the valley. Near the valley floor you'll encounter oaks again; the forest is more spacious, allowing some of them to grow to a massive girth. Bouldery streambeds (some of them slippery; watch your footing!) lie at regular intervals. Soon the way is again lit up by flowers.

Eventually you cross a refreshing stream, the **Ruisseau de Scala** (4h), lined by some splendid old chestnuts. Fifteen minutes later pass through a small chestnut grove. Don't be surprised to encounter livestock and even some wild pigs along the path. The waymarking may have vanished by now, but the contouring route is very obvious, and you need not watch out for any turn-off.

The **Bocca di Lucca** (589m/1932ft; ❹; **4h50min**) is a good viewpoint towards Galéria's gulf — and all the

The Fango

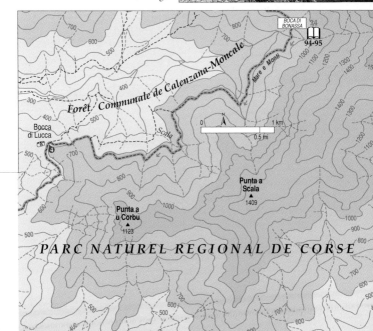

way back to the Bocca di Bonassa. Head left (southeast) over the pass. The next junction comes up at another SADDLE (331m/ 1085ft; **6h**): keep straight ahead here. Tuarelli soon appears below on the river flat. Old stone walls give it a touch of charm.

Within 15 minutes you meet a lane: turn right, towards the hamlet. Cross the bridge (**Pont de Tuarelli-Chiorna**; **❺**; **6h15min**) to meet your taxi on the D351. Take a look at the crystal-clear pool below this bridge; you may not be able to resist jumping into this Olympic-sized waterhole. But if you've asked the taxi to collect you at the idyllic Auberge l'Alzelli (**❻**) on the north side of the bridge (only open May-September), you can always take a dip there...

Ponte Vecchiu (Short walk): the Fango River cuts through the valley floor, leaving many lovely green-tinted rock pools along its course.

Walk 25: BARGHIANA • BOCCA DI CAPRONALE • BARGHIANA

Distance/time: 14km/8.7mi; 7h20min

Grade: ●‡ very strenuous, with a climb of 1000m/3300ft. Cold and dangerous in bad weather. Possibility of vertigo — *and of landslides.* Only recommended for experienced and hardy hikers; *no waymarking.*

Equipment: as page 50; walking boots and warm clothing recommended; *IGN map 4149 OT*

Access: 🚗 car to/from Barghiana (41.5km from Calvi via the airport route). From the village continue by car on the rough track (D351) just at the left of the church and cemetery. Park at the Ponte di e Rocce (3.5km; 42° 20.606'N, 8° 48.150'E). If you're not in a 4WD vehicle, check your insurance for tyre damage — although most people do drive here in normal hire cars.

Short walk/picnic suggestion: Ruisseau de Campottoli Rossi (5km/3mi; 1h30min; ● easy ascent of 160m/525ft on a track). Follow the main walk to the 45min-point (❶), where a small footbridge crosses a cascading stream, and return the same way. Picnic by the stream.

The rewards for this walk will cost you dearly, so save the next day for the beach! This little-frequented footpath climbs through a pleasant evergreen oak forest, following an old mule trail to the Niolo Plateau. Out of the woods, you come to the end of the valley and find that you're completely walled in! Sheer mountains tower above you. But your spectacular onward trail takes you up and over these walls, along precipitous ledges. In all my hiking on Corsica, only on these summits have I spotted the rare moufflon, but I have to confess it's usually only their bums, as they vanish amidst the rock. Good luck!

The walk begins above **Barghiana**, at the **Ponte di e Rocce** (❍; limited parking, in shade). Continue along the track, behind the sign 'CIRCULATION INTERDIT'. As the track bends south after 1km, you have a wonderful view towards the towering peaks of the Cinto range. The **Ruisseau de Capronale**, a tributary of the Fango, flows below you. Soon Capu Tafunatu (2335m/7660ft) catches your eye. A gaping hole the size of a tennis court pierces the peak. According to one legend, the devil bragged to St Martin that he could build a bridge over the torrents of the Golo in a single night. All was complete bar the keystone, when a shepherd in prayer disturbed a nearby cock, causing it to crow. In a fit of rage, the devil hurled his hammer in the air. It flew straight through Capu Tafunatu and landed just off the west coast — forming the Girolata Gulf…

The track narrows to a path and the gushing **Ruisseau de Campottoli Rossi** is crossed on a footbridge (❶; **45min**). *(The Short walk turns back at this delightful spot.)* Continue up the path, after about 30 minutes passing the remains of the old CANTON HOUSE, set back in the trees above the path, just beyond a small bubbly stream. Animal tracks make the route a bit confusing, but there *is* one main mule trail. Pass a SPRING (❷) on your left 15 minutes up from the canton house.

The valley terminates in sheer curving walls just up ahead. Crossing the valley floor, you get a view back onto the rose-coloured hills of the Cinto range. And then the *real* climb begins. The path ascends in sweeping zigzags, frequently interrupted by animal paths cutting straight up the sides of the slopes. Stretches of scree will slow you up. It's more than likely, too, that you'll have to squeeze past timid cows and calves grazing the narrow ledges. Please go *very quietly,* and give them 'right of way'.

Finally you reach the PASS (**Bocca di Capronale**; 1329m/ 4360ft; ❸; **3h45min**). The prominent peak to the north is Punta Silvareccia (1964m/6442ft). The path continues round the valley to the Niolo. As lovely as this vista may be, your eyes will always return to those red hills.

From here return the same way, taking the steep gravelly descent slowly. If it's not too late when you get back to the **Ponte di e Rocce** (**7h20min**), how about a dip in one of the Fango's inviting rock pools?

Capu Tafunatu and the towering walls of the Cinto massif

Distance/time: 13km/8mi; 6h

Grade: ●❟ very strenuous, with an ascent of 750m/2460ft. You must be sure-footed and have a head for heights. Not recommended in changeable weather. Little shade.

Equipment: as page 50; walking boots, sun protection, bathing things, *plenty of water* recommended (no springs en route); *IGN map 4150 OT*

Access: Unless you are travelling with friends/taxi who can not only take you to Galéria early in the morning but collect you on the D81 late in the afternoon, this walk demands an overnight stay at one of the inns or the *gîte d'étape* at Girolata (*book well in advance!*). I suggest getting to the church car park at Galéria with friends/taxi (42° 24.550'N, 8° 38.859'E). Stay overnight at Girolata and return to Calvi by boat the next day. The Colombo Line (Timetable 11; www.colombo-line.com) sails to Calvi from Girolata via the Scandola Reserve between 15.00-16.00; all arrangements can be made at their kiosk at Quai Landry in Calvi (tel: 04 95 65 32 10). Otherwise, if you are *very fit* and you *can* arrange for someone to collect you, carry on from Girolata up to the Bocca di a Croce on the D81 (⑥; allow 2h and another 300m/1000ft of overall ascent from Girolata).

Shorter walk: Chemin du Facteur (10km/6.2mi; 3h40min; ● easy-moderate, with overall ascents of about 550m/1800ft). 🚌 to/from the **Bocca di a Croce** (⑥; on the D81 north of Osani; 42° 19.592'N, 8° 37.943'E). Stout shoes will suffice, but take ample sun protection and bathing things. *Don't miss this walk!* Try to arrive at Girolata before 11.30 or after 14.00, when the excursion boats are not there. The signposted path (the 'Postman's Trail: a well-known local postman walked it every day) begins its descent on the north side of the parking area (with snack bar) at the **Bocca di a Croce** (⑥). It's a variation of the 'Mare e Monti' trail and is waymarked in orange. You pass a SPRING on the descent (❼; 15min). Near the beach, just before a stone wall bordering the path, turn off the 'Mare e Monti' and drop down to the Ruisseau de Tuara and **Plage de Taura** (❽; 40min). Continue alongside another wall and cross another streambed. As you come back into scrub, you meet the 'Mare e Monti' again, at a junction. Take the inland route here, straight up the ridge. When a path (also 'Mare e Monti') joins from the right (35min), keep straight on over the ridge and descend to **Girolata** (❺; 25min downhill; 1h40min). Allow 2h for the return, which you can vary by taking the coastal route back to Tuara (see map; orange waymarks).

The invigorating boat journey to Galéria makes this walk unique on Corsica. (It can be a little choppy, so hopefully you have 'sea legs'!) From the port of Calvi superb coastal scenery follows you all the way, from the citadel, via the red cliffs of the Punta Scandola and the maquis-wooded hills that slip off into the sea, to the sheer mountains of granite bursting up out of the Girolata Gulf. Girolata is a beautifully-sited, rustic tourist-trap only accessible by boat or on foot. (You'll see postcards and pictures of it all round the island.) Excursion boats disgorge day-trippers here for a two-hour lunch before returning. However, once the tourists have gone, peace reigns again, and the natural beauty of this tiny fishing port can be really appreciated.

The walk begins in the characterful old centre of **Galéria**, with the church, *mairie, poste* and a few restaurants. (The rest of this beach-orientated village — except for the UNESCO-protected Fango Delta — is a touristic hodge-podge). Walk out of the CAR PARK (❍) and follow the narrow road on the west side of the

Girolata

CHURCH, with the APSE and BELL TOWER behind you. You immediately pass a wall on the left with signs for 'GIROLATA' and 'GÎTE', as well as an orange waymark. Follow the road past the *gîte* and continue until an orange arrow and a sign, 'TMM' (Tra Monti e Mare) alerts you to where your PATH TURNS OFF LEFT (❶). Stone walls flank your route briefly, before it disappears into woods. Fifteen minutes along you encounter two forks, a minute apart: keep right at the first and left at the second, to cross the **Ruisseau de Tavulaghiu** (❷; **1h**).

Just over the valley floor you rise to a junction. Your way is to the right, and you pass above a muddy RESERVOIR cradled in the valley floor. The cacophony of chorusing frogs is almost deafening. About 15 minutes from the reservoir, you begin a series of stream crossings over the Tavulaghiu (take care on the slippery rocks). Trees draped with vines and creepers shade the way. By now you are steadily ascending up into the high surrounding hills, and despite the zigzags in the path, this stretch is very strenuous. A ROCK BALCONY (**2h15min**) makes a good resting place and viewpoint: you have uninterrupted vistas over the Galéria Gulf and the neighbouring bay. Galéria itself sits back off the shore. The slope is covered in junipers, and in early summer the last of the thorny broom florets add their cheerful colour and delightful fragrance.

Twenty minutes uphill from the viewpoint, you mount the summit of this bumpy ridge and begin to descend along it, accompanied by views to the central massif. Monte Cinto (2706m/8875ft), the island's highest peak, stands head and shoulders above the rest. A brief climb follows, up to a grassy PLATEAU (❸; **Punta di a Literniccia**; **2h50min**), lightly wooded in holm oaks. Go right at the signposted fork here, remaining on the crest of the ridge. (A left turn leads to ⓐ — the Palmarella Pass on the main road.)

Soon the Girolata Gulf comes into sight far below. This exquisite setting is dramatised by a twin-breasted sheer mountain (Monte Seninu, 619m/2030ft) that rears straight up out of the sea and forms the left arm of the bay. The tiny port

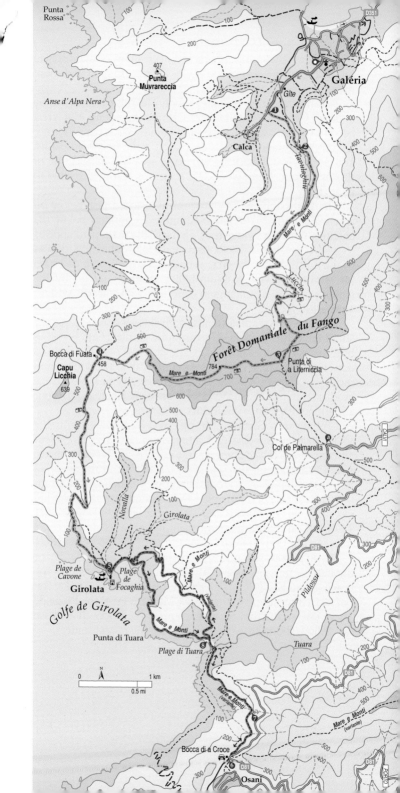

of Girolata sits comfortably tucked in cushions of maquis-clad hills. Beyond the arm of the bay lies the Porto Gulf and more mountains rising from the sea.

Red-tiled rooftops reveal Girolata. The ridge is crowned by a large Genoese watchtower. Clambering along the crest becomes rather awkward and slow-going. Watch your footing; it's very rocky, and the cliffs drop away quite steeply in places. You go from waymark to waymark, weaving in and out of thorny broom. More wonderful seascapes follow, this time to your right.

The highest point in the climb is reached just below an antenna (784m/2570ft; **4h**). Roughly 15 minutes below the antenna, the path swings back on itself: the main path appears to go left here, but in fact loops back sharply to the right to cross to the north side of the crest yet again. At the **Bocca di Fuata** (❹; **4h30min**) you pass through a clearing and go by the remains of a stone building on your right with a nearby WHEAT-THRESHING FLOOR.

From here the path descends south along a side-ridge, to the left of the **Capu Licchia**. The turquoise Girolata Gulf becomes brighter as you descend. You eventually cross over the crest, to descend into a small valley. Leaving this valley, you look across the bay to majestic Mount Seninu. The jagged pink and mauve headland of the Punta Scandola, on your right, holds your attention with its rich colouring.

Coming into **Girolata** (❺; **6h**), you step down through a small cluster of modest pink stone dwellings. The prominent remains of the tower dominate the cove. A few wooden sheds, a lean-to restaurant/bar, and even a stable sit in the shade of scruffy eucalyptus trees around the cove, enhancing the out-in-the-sticks appeal of this hamlet. The wooden jetties and handful of yachts hint at tourism, but all is quiet before 11.30 or after 14.00. If you enjoy lobster, this is the place to tuck in; Girolata's *other* income derives from lobster-fishing.

If you're continuing from here on foot — the same day or the next — pick up your continuation at the other end of the beach (signposts: BOCCA DI A CROCE, CHEMIN DU FACTEUR). You can take either strand of the Mare e Monti as far as the **Plage de Tuara** (❸), where they rejoin to climb to the **Bocca di a Croce** (❻). Allow about 2h — or 2h15min for the inland route.

Walk 27: CAPANDULA CIRCUIT

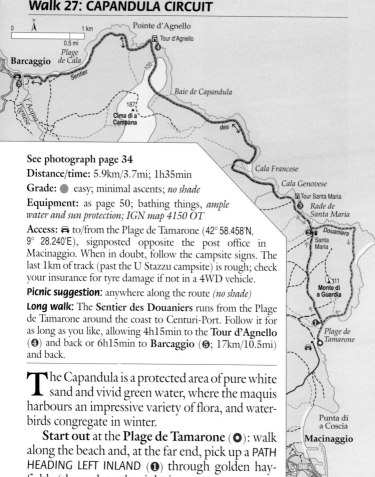

See photograph page 34

Distance/time: 5.9km/3.7mi; 1h35min

Grade: ● easy; minimal ascents; *no shade*

Equipment: as page 50; bathing things, *ample water and sun protection; IGN map 4150 OT*

Access: 🚗 to/from the Plage de Tamarone (42° 58.458'N, 9° 28.240'E), signposted opposite the post office in Macinaggio. When in doubt, follow the campsite signs. The last 1km of track (past the U Stazzu campsite) is rough; check your insurance for tyre damage if not in a 4WD vehicle.

Picnic suggestion: anywhere along the route *(no shade)*

Long walk: The **Sentier des Douaniers** runs from the Plage de Tamarone around the coast to Centuri-Port. Follow it for as long as you like, allowing 4h15min to the **Tour d'Agnello** (❹) and back or 6h15min to **Barcaggio** (❺; 17km/10.5mi) and back.

The Capandula is a protected area of pure white sand and vivid green water, where the maquis harbours an impressive variety of flora, and water-birds congregate in winter.

Start out at the **Plage de Tamarone** (❶): walk along the beach and, at the far end, pick up a PATH HEADING LEFT INLAND (❶) through golden hay-fields (the path to the right is your return route). You cross the low maquis-clothed hills shown on page 34. The tiny **Chapelle Santa Maria** (❷; **30min**) was founded in the 11th century and restored in the 1700s. Not much further on are the intriguing slate-green remains of the grand Genoese **Tour Santa Maria** (❸). It appears to have been sliced down the centre and sits off the shore on a partially-submerged rock. Another watchtower adorns the largest of the Finocchiarola Islands just to the southeast. A short way further along the track, you'll find a lovely SANDY COVE, ideal for swimming.

Returning, fork left just before the chapel on the **Sentier des Douaniers** (Customs Officers' Path; waymarked), to circle back to the **Plage de Tamarone** (**1h20min**).

See also photographs on page 110

Distance/time: 5km/3mi; 2h

Grade: ● short, steep climb of 277m/ 910ft on good paths (orange way-marking)

Equipment: as page 50; *IGN maps 4347 OT, 4348 OT*

Access: 🚌 or 🚐 to/from Lavasina (Timetable 14) on the D80, south of Erbalunga

Photograph: Convento di Capoccini, Pozzo

P oretto and Pozzo are two enchanting villages, surrounded by a tangle of olive and oak trees. If you don't mind a short, stiff climb, this walk is a gem. At the top you can relax with a drink in Pozzo's square and enjoy the 'balcony' view, before returning to the coast.

Begin the walk in **Lavasina**. Head straight up the alley at the left of the 17th-century CHURCH (**O**; **Notre-Dame-des-Grâces**). Continue on a path until you can turn right at a T-JUNCTION (**❶**). Go left at the Y-FORK 100m/yds further on. Cross the D54 (**❷**), go straight ahead on a stepped mule track, then turn right at the next T-JUNCTION (**❸**).

Soon you're in **Poretto**, on a driveway. Some 35m/yds uphill, go right along a lane and, within a minute, turn LEFT UP STEPS (**❹**). Cross a lane and take the first right-hand turn between the houses. Beyond the CHURCH, when the lane swings right, leave it to continue head on a PATH (**❺**). Pass steps climbing to the left and then an impressive FOUNTAIN. When you reach the D54 again, turn right downhill. After 80m/yds, fork left up a CONCRETE LANE (**❻**). When it ends, follow an uphill path between high stone walls.

You come out beside the CHURCH shown above. Continue along the alley towards the door of the adjacent **Convento di Capoccini** (**❼**), but climb steps on the left just before reaching it. Cross the D54 and follow a mule trail to the village road, then turn left to the square in **Pozzo** (**❽**; **1h10min**).

Return the same way to **Lavasina** (**2h**).

Walk 29: MONTE STELLO

See also photograph opposite   **Distance/time:** 13km/8mi; 7h
Grade: ● strenuous, with an ascent of 1030m/3380ft. Recommended for experienced mountain walkers *only*; don't attempt in changeable weather.
Equipment: see page 50; walking boots, warm clothing, ample sun protection and plenty of water recommended; *IGN map 4347 OT*
Access: 🚌 to/from Pozzo, reached via the D54 from either Erbalunga or Lavasina. Or on foot from Lavasina (see Walk 28 opposite).

Monte Stello (1307m/4290ft), long thought to be the highest peak on Cap Corse, is in fact 15m/50ft lower than nearby Cima di e Folicce. Nevertheless, it offers superb views out over the cape. There *is* one catch. Monte Stello is not very generous in sharing this panorama; it's inclined to stay hidden by the mists that so often envelop these summits. The spine of the cape is a bleak and unfriendly landscape so, since you're climbing for the view from the top, make sure it's a glorious day!

The walk begins in the village square in **Pozzo** (●): follow the sign 'MONTE STELLU 4H' and orange flashes, stepping up between the exceptionally neat houses and paved alleyways. Skirting the back of Pozzo, you meet a crossing track. Follow it to the left for a few minutes, then turn right up your stepped path (❶; SIGNPOST). Head straight up onto hillsides overgrown with maquis. If you have seen the 'Attention — feu' signs everywhere, you'll not be surprised to see blackened trees and shrubs covering the slopes. Your first landmark is a DERELICT STONE COTTAGE (**20min**). Go through a stone wall just beyond it and, eight minutes further up, pass below the remains of another stone building.

The trail rises gradually to the west, eventually on the north slopes of the **Ruisseau d'Arega**. You climb past a delicious SPRING (❷; it lies just beyond a water tank), to reach the

*Pozzo's old wash-house;
below: the church in
Lavasina*

Bergerie de Teghime (❸; **2h15min**), sheltering against an outcrop of rock. This is a pleasant spot to get your breath back and quench your thirst before the final assault. From here on, a sharp eye is needed to follow the cairns and orange waymarking, both of which may be obscured by the maquis. Your continuation heads off between the two fenced-off enclosures at the *bergerie*. You ascend to a pass, the **Bocca di Santa Maria** (❹; **3h20min**).

Over the pass, you look down to a bowl-shaped valley and the small village of Piazza, well concealed from the coast. The arid hills of the Désert des Agriates rise beyond Sant-Florent's shimmering blue gulf. Then Monte Stello, a sprawling rocky hill rising out of this backbone of schist, appears to the right. Not far downhill you come to two junctions with trails off to the left: first to a chapel (❺), next to Olmeta/Nonza (❻); keep right at both. Now the summit is just over 200m/650ft above you.

The trail heads directly towards the peak, then rounds it to make the final approach from the north (passing a yellow/red waymarked trail to Silgaggia off left, not all of which is shown on our map). The SUMMIT of **Monte Stello** (❼; **4h**) is a fantastic viewpoint over Cap Corse. Bare rocky hills topple off this wavy mountain range, rolling into the sea on either side of you. On the clearest days your view stretches to the many of the island's other summits. To the east and not far below lie the scattered villages of Sisco (swallowed up in greenery) and (further along the coast) Marine de Pietracorbara.

After returning the same way, end the day by popping in to the friendly café in **Pozzo**'s SQUARE (**7h**).

Walk 30: CORTE • GORGES DU TAVIGNANO • REFUGE DE LA SEGA • CORTE

Distance/time: 32km/20mi; 9h15min

Grade: ●● strenuous and long, with a total ascent of about 800m/2300ft, *much of it in full sun*. You must be sure-footed and have a head for heights. It can be very cold and wet; don't attempt in uncertain weather.

Equipment: as page 50; walking boots, sun protection, warm clothing, bathing things, *ample food and water* recommended; *IGN map 4250 OT*

Access: 🚌 to/from the 'Mare a Mare Nord' signpost, where the walk begins (see 🚌→ on the map). From the centre of Corte, head south on the main street towards Ajaccio, passing the citadel on your right. Just before the bridge over the Tavignano, turn right and follow the Chemin de Baliri, below the citadel, to the waymarked path (paid parking further round to the right; 42° 18.487'N, 9° 8.847'E). Or 🚂 to Corte (Timetable 21); return on the same train (adds 5km/1h15min to the total walking times).

Shorter walk: Gorges du Tavignano (19km/11.8mi; 5h; ● easy-moderate, but still quite long, and with an ascent of 400m/1300ft). Access and equipment as main walk. Follow the walk to the bridge over the Tavignano (❸; **Passerelle Russulinu**; 2h45min) and return the same way. *An ideal day out, highly recommended!*

Alternative, two-day walk: Corte — Refuge de la Sega — Bocca a l'Arinella — Funtana d'Argento — Corte (41km/25.5mi; 12h30min; ●● very strenuous and very long, with a total ascent of about 1300m/4265ft). Only suitable for fit and experienced hikers. It can be very cold and wet; don't attempt in uncertain weather. Plan for an overnight stay at the Refuge de la Sega. There is a guardian from June to October, and food is available, but cooking facilities are also provided. To make a booking, telephone 06 10 71 77 26 (both B&B and half-board offered).

Follow the main walk to the **Refuge de la Sega** (❺). The next day, continue north on the Mare a Mare Nord, still following orange waymarks. You pass below a bare granite hillside, cross a stream, and rise past a lovely waterfall, through a profusion of lily-like sea daffodils (*Pancratium maritimum*). Some 350m/1150ft above the refuge you pass alongside the **Bergerie de Boniacce** (❻; **1h05min**), a shepherds' outpost with a SPRING at the left of the buildings. Bear left on the track just above the *bergerie*, and rejoin your path some 60m/yds uphill, on the right. Cross another track 10 minutes later. In another 10 minutes you reach the **Bocca a l'Arinella** (❼; **1h25min**): just over this pass, an unsurpassed sight greets you — a sweeping view over the immense Golo Valley and across the 'kingdom' of the Niolo, an isolated and very traditional region of Corsica. This is the turning back point for the hike; home is all downhill!

Return to the last track you crossed and follow it to the left. Ignore a rough track to the right and, later, an orange-waymarked path signposted to Corte forking left (it is easier to stay on the track). You pass a HUT on the left (**2h15min**). Some 1h10min along the track (❽; **2h55min**), *watch for your turn-off*: fork left where the track makes a *very sharp bend to the right* (by a small construction, perhaps a sealed reservoir). Now a narrow waymarked path leads you into a magnificent forest of towering Corsican pines, the **Forêt Domaniale du Tavignano**. In a few minutes you cross two small streams; then keep right, round the hillside. Ignore a fork off left within 10 minutes. Some 30 minutes later, just beyond a FORESTRY HOUSE (❾), you will be back on the track. If your bottles need refilling, head *right* on the track for a couple of minutes, to the **Funtana d'Argento**; otherwise go *left* for a few metres/yards, to pick up the continuing path on your right; *take care:* it's rough, steep and overgrown. You rejoin the outward route at the **Passerelle Russulinu** (❸; **5h15min**); follow it back to **Corte**, 2h15min away (**7h30min; 12h30min** overall).

In summer, the most memorable feature of this walk is the lake-sized pool that sits behind the Refuge de la Sega. Tearing yourself away from it is almost impossible; all the day-trippers make a mad dash to catch the last train. Before you reach the refuge, you wind up a gorge, dwarfed by lofty rock walls. Below you lie other tantalisingly beautiful pools.

By car or on foot, approach the starting point for the walk along the CHEMIN DE BALIRI; it follows the Tavignano. The old citadel crowns the hilltop above on your right in a precarious fashion. As the road completes the circuit of the citadel by bending right, turn left on a short access road to an apartment block (you'll see the orange flashes of the 'Mare a Mare Nord'

here). **Begin the walk** from the CAR PARK (**O**): follow the path sign-posted 'REFUGE DE SEGA, PASSE-RELLE RUSSULINU').

Five minutes later, be careful to follow the orange marks up to the right. Soon the old mule trail is circling some hillside terracing. At a FORK (**1**) about 1.5km uphill, again follow the orange waymarks to the right. (The left-hand path drops down to some splendid swimming spots if you follow the riverbed for a little over 30 minutes. And it is possible to scramble steeply back up to the main path further on.)

The riverbed is a string of beryl-green pools. The valley narrows, and the landscape becomes more dramatic, with rocky salients piercing the pine-studded walls. Landmarks are few but, when you pass a STONE HUT (**2**) with a corru-gated iron roof in the **Antia Valley**, you're more than halfway to the bridge (Shorter walk). Emerging from this valley, you come to a prominent rocky belvedere and, some 50 minutes later, you cross the **Tavignano** on the **Passerelle Russulinu** (**3**; **2h45min**) — not a jungle-adventure suspension bridge like some others in this book, but a sturdy bridge with wooden railings.

The Shorter walk turns back at this scenic spot, but over the bridge the main walk veers slightly left at first, before turning right above the river. A tough ascent follows. Looking through the trees onto bare rocky summits, you'll notice a thin veil of green lichen covering these heights. The impressive dome of the Capu Aleri (1634m/5360ft) stands out at the right of the valley. Under an hour above the bridge you encounter a 15-minute stretch of path which is quite precipitous; take special care here if it's wet underfoot. After crossing the **Ruisseau de Castag-nolu** (❹), ignore the fork to the left.

Beyond a tiny reservoir in the river, the way mostly contours, and the valley floor is wider. Passing through moss- and lichen-covered rock, you come upon the **Refuge de la Sega** (❺; **5h**) and the pool shown on page 112, an exquisite beauty spot.

Moving on, the same day or the next, the main walk returns to **Corte** along the same route (**9h15min**).

Walks 31 and 32: Capu a Chiostru, from the Pont de Grotelle

Walk 31: LAC DE MELO AND LAC DE CAPITELLO

See also photograph opposite
Distance/time: 7km/4.3mi; 4h30min
Grade: ● strenuous, but short, with a steep ascent/descent of 560m/1835ft. Dangerous if wet. It can be very cold; don't attempt in unpredictable weather. There are *two routes* up to the lakes (see text below).
Equipment: as page 50; walking boots, sun protection, warm clothing and bathing things recommended; *IGN map 4251 OT*
Access: 🚗 car to/from the Bergeries de Grotelle at the top of the Restonica road (D623), 15km from Corte. This paying car park (42° 13.731'N, 9° 1.826'E) is always busy, so arrive early — or you may have to park well downhill.
Shorter walk/picnic suggestions: *Lac de Melo* (4km/2.5mi; 2h15min; ● fairly strenuous ascent/descent of 340m/1120ft). Follow the main walk to the first lake and picnic there. Or picnic just 30 minutes up the path, at the grassy area by the Restonica (1h return).

Whether you are a walker or not, do make the effort to see the Lac de Melo. It's picture-postcard perfect. The whole Restonica Valley is a wealth of superb scenery, with overpowering peaks, cascading streams, and spell-binding glacial lakes. The aching muscles may not be so memorable, but your photographs surely will.

The walk begins at the **Bergeries de Grotelle** (**O**; car park, drinks and cheese for sale). Follow the signpost 'MELO/ CAPITELLO'; yellow paint marks the route. At the outset, you look straight up at the Capu a Chiostru ridge on your right (see opposite). The Rotondo massif rises to the left. Stands of bright green alders illuminate the rocky inclines. Thorny broom and foxgloves keep you company, as does the thunder of streams crashing down the mountainsides.

Several minutes past the **Bergerie de Melo** (**❶**; selling snacks), you reach a FORK MARKED BY A LARGE CAIRN (**❷**; **30min**). From here there are *two* routes up to the Lac de Melo. It's a somewhat easier ascent to take the path to the *left* here (yellow flashes, cairns). This immediately crosses a grassy area (a fine picnic spot) and then the **Restonica**. In spring, however, the river may be too full to cross.

But let's take the more adventurous main route for the ascent: this keeps to the right of the Restonica and heads up over bare rock. Not long before mounting the saddle, you can either haul yourself up with CHAINS or use the sturdy METAL LADDERS (**55min**). You eventually cross a pass and find yourself in an amphitheatre of rock. A few steps further on you're at the **Lac de Melo** (**❸**; **1h15min**), a dark green mirror filling the basin floor. Nearby lies the perfect picnic spot, a grassy slope shaded by alders. *(The Shorter walk ends here.)*

The Lac du Capitello lies just above the cascading stream you can see on the right-hand side of the mountain walls. Relocate the yellow paint (**❹**; by the tiny STONE SHELTER for the forestry

Lac de Melo (top); there is usually livestock on the Restonica road, so drive carefully!

administration) and climb straight up the steep mountainside. Remain on the right-hand side of the stream for the first 30 minutes. Crossing the stream is a little tricky, and an 'all-fours' climb follows. Red in the face, you squeeze through a gap in the hillside to find the **Lac du Capitello** (**5**; **2h30min**), an indigo-blue pool ensconced in a 40m/130ft-deep hollow. The **Capu a i Sorbi** (2267m/7435ft) flanks it on the right. You can sit here for hours getting drunk on the intoxicating scenery.

Returning, you can take the other route: cross the **Restonica** (**6**) at the Lac de Melo and descend beside the right-hand valley wall. Then go left at the fork just before the stream and cross the **Restonica** again, to join the main path and return to the **Bergeries de Grotelle** (**4h30min**).

See also photographs on page 114 and opposite (below)

Distance/time: 11km/6.8mi; 4h *return*. If you are travelling with friends/a taxi, you can make this a one way walk either down from the Pont de Grotelle (1h45min) or up from the Pont de Frasseta (2h15min).

Grade: ● moderate; descent/reascent of 300m/1000ft. You must be sure-footed (a few rock-falls to cross). *Can be very cold; don't attempt in unpredictable weather.*

Equipment: as page 50; walking boots, warm clothing, bathing things recommended; *IGN map 4251 OT*

Access: 🚗 car to/from the Pont de Grotelle on the Restonica road (D623, 15km from Corte; 42° 14.220'N, 9° 2.3762'E). Or, if you prefer to walk *uphill* first, park at the Pont de Frasseta (just by the rock pinnacle shown below; see map; 42° 15.682'N, 9° 4.345'E).

Short walk/picnic suggestion: Touring with friends, you can make this a one-way walk, as under 'Distance' above. Picnic and swim at the river.

If you've driven up the Restonica road with your heart set on walking up to the lakes (Walk 31), your heart may sink as you reach the Pont de Grotelle! Even out of season, flocks of walkers — like so many sheep — clog the road, all intent on doing the island's best-known hike. You can't help but wonder whether this path above the river itself was opened as an 'over-flow' or escape route, for those of us who don't like crowds! But even if you *do* go up to the lakes, then come back to this balcony footpath another day — it's a brilliant hike in a grandiose setting, with many places to picnic by the river or throw yourself into one of its emerald-green rock pools.

Start out at the **Pont de Grotelle** (○), in the magical alpine setting shown on page 114. Cross the bridge, then turn right

Monte Leonardo's rocky crown, by the Pont de Frasseta

Tip: If you're driving south from Corte and Venaco on the N193, you'll cross the attractive road bridge shown top left before coming to Vivario. On your return — or another day — be sure to take the older road, *below* this bridge, and park by the old road bridge, the Pont du Vecchio (see map pages 66-67). You'll have a better view of the Vecchio River 30m/100ft below you and can look up to one of Gustave Eiffel's lesser-known works of engineering art — this railway bridge rising 100m/330ft above the river. As you can imagine, travelling by train into the interior is simply spectacular!

on a path (signpost: 'PONT DE FRASSETA'). Ample orange flashes, and some cairns, mark the route all the way to your destination — another bridge a little over 5km downstream. Majestic old pines shade the way and frame your photographs up to the peaks and down to the rushing **Restonica River**. The path undulates for most of the way, sometimes crossing fairly steep rock-falls (where cairns indicate the route if the orange-painted rocks have slipped away). After bumbling over a side-stream on stepping-stone *boulders*, with a WATERFALL up to left (**35min**), cross straight over a track. Soon the path is just beside the RIVER (**50min**), a lovely place to swim or picnic.

When you come to a wide CROSSING PATH (**1h**), follow it to the left, eventually rising to a tiny grassy PLATEAU (**1h10min**). From here the path zigzags steeply downhill, crosses two adjacent streams, and then runs through ferns bright with foxgloves in spring. On the final short ascent, you look straight out at **Monte Leonardo**, the rocky pinnacle shown on page 117. At the top of the climb (**1h30min**), just opposite this monolith, you come to a sign: 'PONT DE GROTELLE', pointing back the way you came. Turn right at this junction. (The path to the left climbs over to the Tavignano Valley.) Follow the gentle zigzags of the path down to the **Pont de Frasseta** PARKING AREA (❶; **1h45min**).

Return to the **Ponte de Grotelle** the same way, allowing 2h15min (**4h**).

Walk 33: SENTIER DU LITTORAL: FROM ST-FLORENT TO PUNTA MORTELLA

Distance/time: 20km/12.4mi, 6h20min *from St-Florent;* 13km/8mi; 4h20min *from the Anse de Fornali*

Grade: ● easy ups and downs on a good coastal path (about 200m/650ft over the entire 20km), but virtually *no shade; adequate sun protection is essential. **Unless the weather is exceptionally dry, you may have to walk some distance inland to ford the Fiume Santu (where the water can reach waist level!).***

Equipment: as page 50; stout shoes, ample sun protection (*essential!*), bathing things and *plenty of water* recommended; IGN map 4348 OT

Access: 🚗 car to/from St-Florent or the Anse de Fornali (saves 2h). By car you can drive along the walking route as far as the 1h-point (❸; 42° 41.289'N, 9° 16.365'E), avoiding a fairly miserable, dusty track walk. But the tracks are bumpy to *very* bumpy (depending on the year and the season), so *check your insurance for tyre damage liability,* unless you're in a 4WD vehicle.

Shorter walk/picnic suggestion: Just follow the main walk for as far as you like and drop down to a cove at any point. But there is virtually *no shade.*

L ike Walk 20, this takes in part of the 'Sentier du Littoral', a coastal path stretching the whole length of the Désert des Agriates, from St-Florent to Ostriconi Beach. The land (5000 hectares/12,000 acres) was bought in the 1990s by the

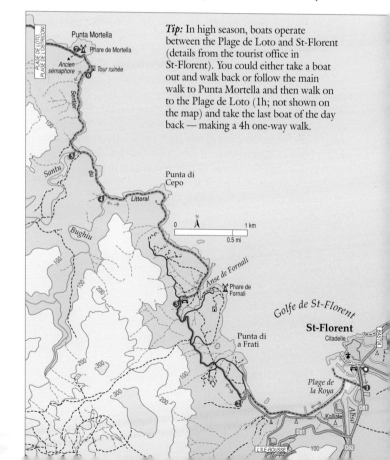

Tip: In high season, boats operate between the Plage de Loto and St-Florent (details from the tourist office in St-Florent). You could either take a boat out and walk back or follow the main walk to Punta Mortella and then walk on to the Plage de Loto (1h; not shown on the map) and take the last boat of the day back — making a 4h one-way walk.

Conservatoire du Littoral and is being developed and managed for the enjoyment of walkers. The whole stretch takes 15 hours, but overnight stops can be made at either Saleccia Beach or Ghignu.

The walk starts in the centre of **St-Florent** (◐): follow the main D81 towards L'ILE-ROUSSE. At the port, take the FOOT-BRIDGE (❶) to the far side of the **Aliso River** and walk across the sandy **Plage de la Roya** to the end. From the end of the beach head inland; then, almost immediately, turn right up a narrow lane, onto a dirt road (❷; **25min**). After a dusty, boring 35 minutes, you'll arrive above the **Anse de Fornali** (❸; **1h**), where the walk proper begins. Here you'll find a signpost for the SENTIER DU LITTORAL. From the parking area head down to the coastal path.

Heading west, you pass below some exquisite properties. But your attention will be no doubt be drawn to the wild flowers, the cloud patterns over Cap Corse, and the endless expanse of crystal-clear aquamarine sea. Just walk as far as you like, ending the short walk with a picnic and swim — preferably in a little inlet all your own. Landmarks are the sandy beach at the mouth of the **Fiume Bughiu** (❹; **2h**) and the fiord-like inlet at the **Fiume Santu** (❺; **2h20min**), where you'll probably have to wade in waist-high water or detour inland! From here it's another 50 minutes to the **Punta Mortella** (❻; **3h10min**), with its old Genoese WATCHTOWER. (Nelson was so impressed when his fleet attacked this very tower in 1794 that the so-called Martello towers in Kent and Sussex were built and named after this one.) About 100 towers — some round, some square — were built along the coast in the 16th and 17th centuries, mostly as a protection against North African invaders. Their fire-signals could go round the whole island in just two hours!

After perhaps going on to the LIGHTHOUSE (❼), return to **St-Florent** the same way (**6h20min**).

Anse de Fornali, where the path proper begins

Walk 34: MONTE SAN PETRONE

Distance/time: 12km/7.5mi; 5h

Grade: ● moderate-strenuous, with an ascent of 780m/2560ft on good tracks and paths, mostly in shade.

Equipment: as page 50; walking boots, warm clothing, and *plenty of water* recommended; *IGN map 4150 OT*

Access: 🚗 car to/from the Col de Prato (42° 25.651'N, 9° 19.867'E), reached via the D71 east from Ponte Leccia, via Morosaglia

Short walk/picnic suggestion: *San Petru d'Accia* (2.5km/1.6mi; 50min; easy; stout shoes will suffice). Follow the main walk to ❶ (the 17min-point). Turn 90° left here, rising past a water tank on the left. The track reaches the chapel **San Petru d'Accia** (❸; half ruined, half new) in 10min — a fine picnic spot. The chapel is surrounded by a wall (to keep out the pigs); take the wide downhill path just at the left side of the wall (as you face the chapel) to descend due north, back to the track, then turn right to the Col de Prato.

O n a clear day you can see as far as the Tuscany from the summit of Monte San Petrone, la Castagniccia's 'sacred' mountain. In fact Christianity was brought to the area from the Tuscan islands and, believe it or not, there was a cathedral near the summit in the 12th century!

The walk begins at the **Col de Prato** (❍): take the track (initially surfaced) heading south almost opposite the sign for the col (*no* walkers' signpost here at time of checking, only an orange flash on an electricity pole at the right). Walk to the right of a snack bar and fencing. Twenty paces past the end of the fencing, a path on the left is your return route. Beyond a PIG STYE (**10min**), at a three-way fork (❶; **17min**), take the middle route, almost straight ahead. *(But for the Short walk, go left.)*

The track rises gently through beech woods. There are more STYES along here, but the pigs are likely to be running free (*beware:* if you feed them, they'll keep following you and can be very aggressive). Soon a stand of magnificent old chestnut trees interrupts the beeches. At another fork (❷; **25min**), take the lower track to the right. At the next fork (❸; **45min**), go left uphill. Ten minutes later, on a RISE in a small pine wood (❹; **55min**), *leave* the track: take the path to the left (the main trail heads right to Saliceto). Your path (red paint waymark on a tree) rises to a flat area.

So far the going has been fairly easy, but now the hard work begins. Climbing steading (again through beech), you pass a spring on the right (**Fontana di e Teghie** (❺; **1h25min**). Keep left at a fork 150m/yds further on. Eventually you rise to a sunny SADDLE (1536m; ❻; **2h05min**) in an alpine setting and enjoy the first long-range views. Ignore the paths to the right at this saddle; your waymarked path contours left (due north) through old pastures before the final assault.

From the SUMMIT of **Monte San Petrone** (1767m/5796ft;

San Petru d'Accia (top) is surrounded by stone walls, to keep out the half-wild pigs Bottom right: at the San Petrone summit

⑦; **2h45min**) the long arm of Cap Corse stretches out in the east beyond the green hills of la Castagniccia; to the west is la Balagna, backed by the summit of Monte Cinto. And beyond the Tuscan archipelago, even the snow-capped Alps can be seen on a clear day.

Return the same way, but visit the chapel of **San Petru d'Accia** (**⑧**; see Short walk) — and from there take the ferny path back to the **Col de Prato** (**5h**).

Walk 35: FOCE FINOSA AND REFUGE DE PALIRI

See map page 125

Distance/time: 8km/5mi; 4h

Grade: ● fairly strenuous ups and downs on rocky paths; overall ascent/descent about 600m/1970ft. Don't attempt in changeable weather; dangerous if wet.

Equipment: as page 50; walking boots, warm clothing, water recommended; *IGN map 4253 ET*

Access: 🚗 car or 🚌 (Timetable 5) to/from the Auberge du Col de Bavella (200m east of the Col de Bavella; 41° 47.742'N, 9° 13.476'E)

Short walk/picnic suggestion: Foce Finosa (●; 5km/3mi; 2h30min; easy-moderate, with an overall ascent/descent of about 310m/1020ft). Follow the main walk for the first 1h15min, to ➎, then return the same way. There's a lovely grassy picnic place just beyond the 10min-point, in the shade of pines, with fine views of the valley.

The Massif of Bavella, with its towering pink walls of jutting crags and magnificent pine forest, has a magnetic, irresistible beauty. And then there are the views … some of the finest on Corsica. On these grassy, cushion-soft inclines that hide amidst the rock, no picnic has ever tasted more delicious.

Start out at the AUBERGE DU COL DE **Bavella** (**O**; **200m** east downhill from the parking area at the col). Take the forestry track opposite the *auberge,* marked with the red and white flashes of the GR20 and signposted 'PALIRI'. There is a FOUNTAIN here. From the outset you have a superb view that stretches to the sea, but it's the formidable wall of rocky pink crags bulging out of the landscape and blocking your way that holds your attention. Pines wood the sheer slopes. From here the modest settlement of Bavella is concealed by woods.

Some 600m/yds from the *auberge* (➊; **10min**), leave the track: fork left on a path (Walk 36 takes the path forking off to the right just before this turning). A steep descent (very slippery when wet) takes you down into a wooded gulley. The inclines are spongy with grass and patched with fern, the pines elegantly tall and straight. This is a lovely picnic setting, with views towards the dramatic, pink-tinted walls of the valley.

The path drops you down onto another TRACK (➋; **40min**), where you turn right. You pass a fork off to the right and soon cross an ebullient stream (➌; **Ruisseau de Volpajola**; you may have to wade across in spring). Minutes over the ford, a signpost (➍; 'REFUGE DE PALIRI') directs you up a path to the right. Zigzag up the steep rocky path to the summits and the **Foce Finosa** (1206m/3960ft; ➎; **1h15min**). *The Short walk turns back here.*

To enjoy the best views from this pass you need to scramble *(with great care)* up onto the crest of the ridge, so that you can see over the pines. The awe-inspiring Aiguilles de Bavella rise inland: massive slabs of rock lining the valley walls dominate the landscape. On the coast lies the Gulf of Porto-Vecchio with its

123

The Bavella massif is an unforgettable picnic setting, dominated by pink-tinted granite cliffs. Above: view towards the Aiguilles de Bavella through trees, on the way to the Pianona viewpoint (the 30min-point in Walk 36). Left: the Refuge de Paliri sits just at the foot of the mighty Punta Tafunata di i Paliri; there's a table and benches in front, or a more sheltered spot just over the ridge to the right.

scooped-out, white-collared bays. In your immediate surroundings, the rock can be anything from a soft pink to a deep rose, depending on the time of day.

Continuing on to the Refuge de Paliri, descend the very steep and rocky hill below the pass, looking straight out to the magnificent Porto-Vecchio Gulf. Fortunately, this jarring descent changes direction and swings left across the flank of the ridge, to meet a junction 35 minutes below the pass. Follow the GR20 up to the left here.

You cross two streams in quick succession (fill up with water at the signposted SPRING here) just below the **Refuge de Paliri** (**6**; **2h**). This small alpine retreat comes as a pleasant surprise. Built of stone, with a wooden roof, it could be an up-market shepherds' hut. It shelters on a grassy slope, in the company of a few splendid pines — the whole setting dwarfed by a backdrop of great granite cliffs falling off the shoulders of the **Punta Tafunata di i Paliri**.

When you've tired of this blissfully peaceful spot, return the same way to **Bavella** (**4h**).

Walk 36: TROU DE LA BOMBE

See also photograph opposite (top)   **Distance/time:** 6km/3.7mi; 2h

Grade: ● fairly easy, with overall ascents of under 150m/500ft, but agility is required on the approach to the Trou de la Bombe.

Equipment: see page 50; walking boots are best; *IGN map 4253 ET*

Access: as Walk 35, page 123

Short walk/picnic suggestion: Pianona viewpoint (●; 2.8km/1.7mi; 55min; easy). Follow the main walk to the 30min-point. Then retrace your steps and keep left at both forks, to return to 'Bavella par la Chapelle'.

This walk to the edge of the southern Bavella massif is shady and undemanding — a perfect outing for a warm day. But it's not lacking in drama — you can either admire the 'shell-hole' from a distance, or climb up to it!

Start out by following WALK 35 (page 123). About 600m from the *auberge*, fork right uphill (❶; **10min**) on a red/orange-waymarked path (30 paces before Walk 35 forks left). This rises gently through ferns and pines. Ten minutes uphill pass a path off right (red/orange waymarks) signposted 'BAVELLA PAR LA CHAPELLE' (❷; your return route). Go straight on here (red waymarks; signposted 'PIANONA', 'COMPULEDDU'). Two minutes later, at a Y-fork, 'COMPULEDDU' is signed down to the left. Although that is our destination, first we'll make a short detour.

Fork *right uphill* here for 'PIANONA' (orange waymarks). An easy ascent of eight minutes brings you to a crossing track at the top of a rise, at the setting shown opposite. The trees are too high here: walk just over 100m/yds to the right, to the **Pianona VIEWPOINT** — a clearing by a telecoms mast, for a good view to the Aiguilles de Bavella (❸; **30min**).

Return past where you joined the track and, 300m/yds further on, fork left on a lesser track (❹; *not* waymarked). This narrows to a path and brings you back to the main red-waymarked path in four minutes: turn right on this wider, crossing path. The gently undulating path brings you to a barrage of signposts at the **Bocca di Velaco** (❺; **55min**). Cairned paths (*not* signposted) lead almost straight ahead from this pleasant clearing up to the jagged heights of Punta Velaco and Le Promontoire. But we turn *left* here (red waymarks). After about seven minutes, take a path climbing up to the right (red waymarking on trees). In two minutes you're just below the 'shell-hole' (**❻**; **Trou de la Bombe**; **1h05min**). Red flashes show the best way to the hole itself, if you're very agile … and brave.

Back at the Bocca di Velaco, retrace your outgoing route (it may be signed 'BAVELLA PAR LA CHAPELLE'). Just after crossing a stream, you are back at the sign for the Pianona detour. Go right, then, two minutes later, fork left (**❷**), now following red and orange flashes to the **Chapelle de la Sainte Vierge** (**❼**; **1h50min**) and on to **Bavella** (**2h**).

Trou de la Bombe (i Tafunu di u Compuleddu in Corse)

Walk 37: CASCADE DE PISCIA DI GALLO

Distance/time: 4.7km/2.9mi; 2h

Grade: ● easy until the final descent to the bottom of the gorge (which requires scrambling on all fours). But it is not necessary to descend this path; you can see the top half of the waterfall from this point. *The descent into the gorge is dangerous in wet weather.* Total descent/ascent of 160m/525ft

Equipment: as page 50; stout shoes will suffice unless you are making the difficult descent which requires walking boots; *IGN map 4254 ET*

Access: 🚗 car or 🚐 (Timetable 5) to/from the large (paid) parking area on the D368 3.5km north of the Barrage d'Ospédale dam wall (41° 41.268'N, 9° 12.037'E). Discouragingly, there are quad bikes for hire here.

Picnic suggestion: Follow the main walk for up to 30min; picnic either at the Oso by the first BRIDGE (❶; 5min) or much further on in the walk, where a side-path (❹) goes down to the stream. Adequate shade.

The Piscia di Gallo waterfall is more striking for its setting than its size, although it does fall 70m/230ft in one sheer drop, shooting straight out of a sheer face of rock. To me the setting is reminiscent of the Orient: a mountain scene painted by a Chinese master.

Start the walk from the PARKING AREA (○) by following 'DEPART CASCADE' and yellow waymarks down to the **Oso Stream** and then walking alongside it. You cross a side stream on a BRIDGE (❶; **5min**) and, about 1km from the start, join a TRACK (❷; **20min**). After another 600m/yds, leave the track: turn left and cross the Oso at a FORD (❸; this may be wet outside summer; in summer the stream may be bone-dry). Over the stream, *watch for a path off to the right,* climbing a rocky surface. (The main path continues straight on before it, too, bends right.) Taking this less-obvious path, you reach a low crest, from where you bear left. A bouldery landscape with heather and pines lies before you. Further along the ridge, you can see a stretch of coastline. A PATH (❹) forks off right here, down to the stream, at a spot where you can usually escape the crowds.

Then the main path comes in from the left, at a clearing used for emergency HELICOPTER LANDINGS (**35min**). The Oso flows in the rocky gulley below you on the right; it later empties into the Gulf of Porto Vecchio. Your way heads across the rock and through the maquis. Livestock paths sometimes cross the path you are following, so keep an eye on the waymarking (... and the rubbish left by the hundreds of walkers who visit these falls every day in summer).

Just before the descent begins you come face to face with TWO ENORMOUS BOULDERS (❺) — one balancing atop the other

— teetering on a 'thread' of rock. The path starts to descend just to the left of them. After a short distance, it bends to the right and becomes steeper. A few minutes later you pass to the right of another very large BOULDER and soon come to a sign, 'PASSAGE DANGEREUX' (**6**; **45min**). The top half of the **Cascade de Piscia di Gallo** is visible from here; it leaps out of a towering rock face and plummets into a gorge of dense vegetation. An impressive sight … but even more so when you're down in the gorge looking up at it.

A very rough, rocky, and steep descent follows. *Take great care. All fours are needed.* You descend under a thick canopy of vegetation, cool and dark. Dropping as far as you can *safely* go (**55min-1h**), you still cannot reach the foot of the falls. You look through trees, to see the waterfall thunder down on to the rocks below, where three gushing arms of water cascade into a pool.

On your return, after coming back to the TWO BALANCING BOULDERS (**5**), it is possible to descend to the river and follow it upstream, before climbing up to your original route near the HELICOPTER LANDING SITE. Then return to the CAR PARK (**2h**).

WALK 38: MONTE CALVA AND THE 'DIAMOND'

Distance/time: 7km/4.3mi; 3h (with optional detour to the Bergerie de Luviu 12km/7.5mi; 4h30min; see footnote on page 130)

Grade: ● easy-moderate, with an ascent of 400m/1290ft; stony underfoot

Equipment: as page 50; walking boots and sunhat recommended; *IGN map 4254 ET*

Access: 🚗 car or 🚌 (Timetable 5) to/from the Bocca d'Illarata (D368, 10km north of l'Ospédale; 41° 42.312'N, 9° 12.674'E)

Short walk/picnic suggestion: Punta di u Diamanti (easy; about 25min). See notes from the 2h35min-point overleaf. Fine picnic spots.

This walk is at its best on a clear day in spring or autumn. Monte Calva may not be an inspiring peak to climb, but from the top you will look out west as far as the Golfe de Valinco, while the eastern gulfs seem to lie at your feet. Then round off the walk in the foothills of the Punta di u Diamanti, which *is* an inspiring peak, as shown below.

Begin on the track opposite the sign 'BOCCA D'ILLARATA' (a WALKERS' INFORMATION BOARD is to the right). Ignoring any offshoots, always keep straight ahead on the cairned main track. It rises gradually and becomes eroded. Churned-up earth gives away places where wild pigs have been rooting for food.

When the trees thin out (**40min**), there are wonderful views back over to the Punta di u Diamanti rising above the pass. Five minutes later you pass the rock pillars shown overleaf and then come to a large CAVE on the right (**50min**). Ignore a path off left one minute past the cave (❶) but, seven minutes later, where the track bends right, turn sharp left up a footpath marked by a large CAIRN (❷). (But keep *right* if you would like to visit the Bergerie de Luviu. The track we've been following, bulldozed over an old footpath, leads to this isolated outpost in the pines some 2.5km away, for which you should allow 1h30min return.)

The rocky facets of the aptly-named Punta di u Diamanti

From now on you find yourself in a 'museum' of cairns, as paths thread their way left uphill, towards a gigantic red-rock cairn on a rocky outcrop. Struggling up the stony shoulder, you pass to the right of this huge cairn and come to a TV antenna. Just to the left is the TRIG POINT on the **Monte Calva** SUMMIT (❸; **1h30min**). But another 300m/yds along the ridge, you'll come to a SECOND SUMMIT just 4 metres higher…

Return more or less the way you came. In 15 minutes you descend to a small plateau and a Y-FORK (❺). You came up the path to the left. Take the right-hand path to descend; you're back on the track at ❶ in five minutes. Turn right and descend to the **Bocca d'Illarata** (**2h35min**).

Now go down the path behind the 'BOCCA D'ILLARATA' sign on the west side of the pass. The many paths here (some cairned) allow you to ramble or scramble below the **Punta di u Diamanti**. Allow about 25 minutes (**3h**).

Walk 39: FORET DE L'OSPEDALE

See map opposite (below) and photograph on page 1

Distance/time: 4km/2.5mi; 1h15min

Grade: ● easy; ascent of 100m/325ft on woodland paths; well waymarked, but *in heavy mist it's best to retrace the yellow-marked path from Foce Alta*

Equipment: no special equipment needed; *IGN map 4254 ET*

Access: 🚗 car to/from the 'Tafoni' trail: 1km north of l'Ospédale, turn left off the D386 for 'Agnarone, Cartalavonu'. See 🚗 → symbols on the map: fork left, left, and left. Park on the right, 500m uphill, at the trail (41° 39.200'N, 9° 10.751'E).

Alternative walks

1 Punta di a Vacca Morta (●; 5km/3mi; 2h; walking boots recommended). Follow the main walk or Alternative walk 2 to Foce Alta, then head up to this rocky peak. Cairning is unreliable; not advisable in heavy mist.

2 Foce Alta from the Col de Mela (●; 4km/2.5mi; 1h10min). Use the map to reach the Col de Mela (41° 39.854'N, 9° 10.586'E) and from there follow the Mare a Mare — taking in the *unmarked, unreliably cairned* path to the Punta di a Vacca Morta if you like. Or follow the Mare a Mare down to Cartalavonu (good food at the *gîte,* Le Refuge) and up the road to the Tafoni path. Pick up the main walk at the 35min-point, then head back to the Col de Mela.

This walk, one of the most beautiful in the south, is perfect for the whole family. Paths soft with pine needles and aglow with cyclamen in spring, take you to a shady plateau with attractively eroded rocks *(tafoni)*, from where the *sportifs* can forge a way up to the cross on 'Dead Cow Peak'.

Start out just to the left of the PARKING BAY (**O**): follow the clear **Sentier des Tafoni**, a lovely Forestry Department nature trail marked by posts showing two balancing rocks, as well as copious yellow flashes and infrequent blue dots. Cross a BRIDGE (**10min**) and five minutes later turn right on a crossing track. But after only 70m/yds, where the track makes a U-turn to the left, go sharp left on the continuation of your path (**❶**). Meeting a second track, turn right for just a few paces and pick up the path again (**❷**; almost opposite). Soon you join the orange-waymarked Mare a Mare, a woodland trail coming from the right; follow it to the left (**35min**).

Watch out, 10 minutes along, for a narrow path down to the left (**❸**; BLUE DOT ON A TREE) — your return route. Two minutes later, SIGNPOSTS point the way right to the Vacca Morte (**❻**), left to Cartalavonu (**❼**) and back the way you've come to the Col de Mela (**❽**) — all possible variations of this walk for which GPS tracks are available. Head left, to find a resting spot here at **Foce Alta** (**❹**; **47min**), among the *tafoni,* pines and tall grasses.

Retrace your steps from the signposts for 120m and turn right down the path marked with *sparse* blue dots. In seven minutes *be sure to turn left downhill* (**❺**; FLUORESCENT ORANGE '⊃' MARKS). Cross the end of a track and head half-right (BLUE/YELLOW WAYMARKS, POST). Quickly joining your outward path, turn right, back to the 'SENTIER DES TAFONI' SIGNPOST (**1h15min**).

131

See also photographs on page 47

Distance/time: 9km/5.6mi; 3h10min

Grade: ● easy; a walk for all the family. Overall ascents/descents of about 300m/1000ft. Can be very windy: on such days *do not* venture near the edge of the cliff! *Almost no shade.*

Equipment: as page 50; stout shoes, bathing things, sun protection and plenty of water recommended; *IGN map 4255 OT*

Access: 🚌 to/from Bonifacio; park by the port (41° 23.348'N, 9° 9.989'E). Or 🚐 (Timetable 19)

Short walk/picnic suggestion: ●Bonifacio cliffs (up to 2.5km/1.5mi; 45min; easy). Follow the main walk for the first 10-25min, to picnic anywhere along the magnificent limestone cliffs. *No shade.*

B onifacio is a must for all visitors to southern Corsica. This dramatically-sited, cliff-hanging town, with its centuries-old narrow streets is most impressive. The walk too, is quite spectacular. Wandering along the windswept cliff-tops on this southernmost tip of the island, you're virtually blinded by the chalk-white limestone bluffs and the dazzling navy blue sea that they overhang.

Begin the walk at the church of **St Erasme** (❍), near the western end of the marina-side cafés in **Bonifacio**. (In the Genoese era this was the fishermen's church, since they were forbidden entry into the town.) Climb the flight of steps towards the old town. Tall, ancient buildings (with facelifts) line the steep pedestrian way. The imposing citadel walls rise high above you, on your right. Five minutes up, a magnificent view awaits you at the **Col St Roch** (❶). You look along the sheer curving coastline of brilliant white cliffs. On clear days you can see the low hills of Sardinia rising in the southeast. The chapel here at the viewpoint marks the site of the death of the last victim of the Great Plague of 1528, which wiped out 60 per cent of the town's population.

To head out around the cliffs, climb the paved path that ascends to the left ('*CIRCUIT PEDESTRE DES FALAISES*'). You have a fine view back towards the strategically-sited town and over into the inlet sheltering the port. Once on the cliffs, hold onto your hats! The paving soon peters out and you're following a worn path of earth and stones. The surrounding peninsula is flat, but endless gulleys (many of them hidden from view) bite into it. Low wind-bent junipers and maquis shade the landscape in dark green hues. Far inland you can see the tail of the Montagne de Cagna.

It's very tempting to peer over the very edge of the cliffs, but *this is exceedingly dangerous*, because there's often a big overhang that could easily crumble away. There are a couple of viewpoints with protective walls; otherwise, keep well back from the edge if it's windy, and supervise children carefully. All the way along you overlook the wind- and sea-eroded coastline — a magnificent picnic setting.

You pass the SHELL OF A BUILDING (**30min**) and 15 minutes later join the LIGHTHOUSE ROAD (**45min**). Turn right here and, when the road forks (**55min**), head right towards the Phare (lighthouse) de Pertusato. Minutes later you circle a small gulley. Strike off right here on a path (**❷**); it takes you down to the edge of the sea in eight minutes, onto smooth white tongues of limestone.

Bonifacio overhangs the sea from its cliff-top perch.

Take the same path back to the road and ascend past GUN BATTERIES and, a little further on, the **Sémaphore de Pertusato** (❸). Crossing a crest, you get a closer look at Sardinia, only twelve kilometres away. The Iles Lavezzi form the necklace of rocky islets between the two islands. The lighthouse sits alone on the point ahead.

Two or three minutes below the crest, just as the road makes a U-turn, ignore a track going almost straight ahead. But, just 20m/yds further on, take a path off left (❹), ascending through the hillside scrub. Squeezing through the thorny maquis, you'll see a wealth of rosemary and red-berried *Lentiscus*. Should you venture upon herds of grazing goats out here, pass them quietly. Five minutes through the scrub you rejoin the road. Turn left and, after 30m/yds, turn hard back to the right on a dirt track. Then, just 40m/yds down the track, take the path descending the left-hand wall of a gulley that cuts down to the shore. A curious piece of coastline eaten away by wind and water awaits you. A monumental salient of limestone dominates the hilly waterfront.

When you reach the water's edge, you discover a small sandy BEACH (**1h30min**), obscured by the rocky shoreline. The small islet of St Antoine, adorned with a cross, hides behind the monumental rock. There's also a steep path from the beach straight up to the LIGHTHOUSE (ⓐ; not included in the walking times). Climb the rock for another fine view of Bonifacio. A BLOWHOLE (❺) lies unnoticed to the right of the rock. Approach the edge with the utmost care, as it, too, is eaten away underneath. Pay particular attention when gale force winds batter the point here!

Return the same way to **Bonifacio** (**3h10min**). In calm weather, you may want to explore some paths to the left of the road, along the shoreline.

Index

Only geographical names are included here. For other entries, see Contents, page 3. *Italic* page numbers indicate a map, **bold** numbers a photograph (either of these may be in addition to a text reference on the same page).